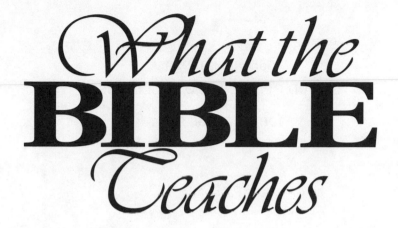

What the BIBLE Teaches

DR. RAYMOND BARBER

SWORD of the LORD
PUBLISHERS
P.O. BOX 1099, MURFREESBORO, TN 37133

Printed and Bound in the United States of America

What the
BIBLE
Teaches

Dedication

This book is affectionately dedicated to the members of Worth Baptist Church, who have so faithfully encouraged me in my endeavor to preach and publish the Word of God.

Their attentiveness to the truth and their love for the Scriptures have inspired me for more than thirty years.

To me, they are the greatest people on earth. May the Lord of Heaven and earth bless them and increase their kind over all the earth.

Raymond W. Barber

Table of Contents

Foreword

The messages in this book were preached in a series of messages in 1973 from the pulpit of Worth Baptist Church, where on January 12, 1992, I celebrated my thirtieth anniversary as pastor.

Covering some of the vital issues and essential doctrines of the Word of God, the messages are designed to bring the truth of the Bible to the hearts of men in a clear and concise manner.

The Bible is our only source of divine inspiration, and from its pages God not only makes known His purpose and plan for the universe, but His design and desire for every member of Adam's race. Thus, these messages were prepared and preached in view of God's revelation to us.

The prayer of my heart is that God will use this book of sermons to bring the lost to Christ and to strengthen the believer in the faith.

Raymond W. Barber

Introduction

Dr. Raymond Barber has been pastor of the Worth Baptist Church in Fort Worth, Texas, since 1962 and president of the Independent Baptist Fellowship International since its inception in 1984. In addition to his pulpit ministry, Dr. Barber has taught preacher boys at a Baptist college for many years. Anyone who hears this man preach is immediately impressed, not only with the content of his sermons but also with the way he outlines his messages.

Dr. Barber is a popular conference speaker. Former editor of *Searchlight*, he has been a featured speaker in our National Sword of the Lord Conferences, and his sermons often appear on the pages of THE SWORD OF THE LORD. We have used a number of his sermons in our GREAT PREACHING series.

Our friend and Board member has done preachers and teachers everywhere a great favor by making these thirteen excellent sermons on important Bible doctrines available. We believe this first book by Raymond Barber will be well received by preachers and laymen as well.

We look forward to publishing other books by this great preacher, which will eventually include outlines on every book in the Bible. Be sure you get every volume. These are books you will refer to time and time again. We recommend that every preacher and Sunday school teacher have his own volume and that additional copies be purchased and given to young ministerial students everywhere.

Curtis Hutson
Editor, SWORD OF THE LORD

1

THE BIBLE

and Inspiration

"**A**ll scripture is given by inspiration of God, and is profitable for doctrine, for reproof, for correction, for instruction in righteousness."—II Tim. 3:16.*

Abraham Lincoln once said, "Take all the Bible that you can by reason and the rest by faith, and you will live and die a better man."

There is in the world an appalling ignorance of the Word of God, even among so-called fundamental Christians.

A teacher once asked a group of children, "What's in the Bible?"

After a moment or two of silence, a little girl raised her hand and said, "I know what's in the Bible. Now let me see. There are a lot of dates, marriages, deaths, clippings from the paper, two valentines, a birthday card, a Christmas card, and that's about all." She knew what was kept in her Bible at home.

The reason people are ignorant of the Word of God is that they do not read it. It would be interesting to take a survey of the average congregation and find out how much time is spent in reading the Word of God from week to week.

A preacher was with a family on one occasion while delivering some special messages in the community. On the first evening he was there, before they retired, he said, "I would like to read from your Bible a few verses of Scripture and have a prayer before we retire." They stammered about and finally found the Bible. When the preacher opened it, out popped a pair of glasses. The mother and wife of the home said before she thought, "Why, I do declare! There are my specs! They've been lost four years, and I haven't been able to find them anywhere."

That is why we are appallingly ignorant of the Word of God. We are not reading. We are not studying. We are not giving ourselves to meditation in the Word of God. Around the world, men and women are hungering for the truth and for righteousness. We have it in the lids of this Book, but the greatest tragedy I know anything about is, we are keeping this priceless treasure God has given us.

Did you know there are over two thousand languages and dialects into which not one single word of the Scripture has ever been translated? We should take that as a challenge and do our part somehow, someway, to reduce the number of languages in which the Bible has never been translated.

The Bible is such a wonderful treasure. It presents the only key we have that opens the door to the revelation of God. It portrays the only Saviour who opens the way to Heaven. It provides the answer to the perplexing problems and questions of life. Every area of human knowledge is touched on in this Book. Not one single field of learning has been left out. The Bible is as up to date as tomorrow morning's newspaper headlines. Old as time and new as tomorrow is the Book of God.

Basic Questions

Certain basic questions arise about the Bible. For example: Where do we get the word *Bible?* Why do we call it *Bible?* *Bible* comes from the Greek *biblos* which means book. By the thirteenth century, the Scriptures were commonly referred to as "the Book." So our word *Bible* in the English comes from the Greek *biblos,* meaning book.

More questions arise, like these: Can we really trust the Bible? Is the Bible really the Word of God? Or is the Bible like the sacred books of other religions? Is it like the *Tripitaka,* for example, of Buddhism? Is it like the *Analects* of Confucianism? Is it like the *Veda* of Hinduism, the *Koran* of Mohammedanism, or the *Avesta* of Zoroastrianism? Is the Bible just another book of another religion that is called sacred by those who follow it? How do we know the Bible is inspired?

Biblical Inspiration

The Bible testifies to its own inspiration. Over 2500 times in this Book the words, *"Thus saith the Lord,"* or, *"The Lord said,"* appear. Now right away some liberal, some modernist, some critic of the Bible will say, "But you can't go into the Bible to prove its own inspiration. You must go outside."

Let me give you an illustration of proving something from within.

Suppose I had a glass of water here on the pulpit desk and wanted to find out chemically the components that go into the water. Wouldn't you think me very foolish if I went down to the service station, got a bottle of gasoline and started probing around in the gasoline to find out what was in the water?

If we are going to go scientifically and logically, we must look within the testimony of the Book itself. After all, the

Book is a "speaking" Word. God has spoken! "Thus saith the Lord," and we dare not add to nor take away from the Holy Writ, the Holy Record, the Holy Book of God.

Testimony of Jesus

Jesus testifies to the inspiration of the Scripture in more than one place, and I give you two references. First, in John 10:35 Jesus said, "The scripture [basically referring to the Old Testament because the New Testament had not been written at that point] cannot be broken." Second, in Matthew 24:35, Jesus said, "Heaven and earth shall pass away, but my words shall not pass away."

Testimony of Peter

The Apostle Peter testifies to the inspiration of the Scriptures, and I read to you II Peter 1:19-21:

"We have also a more sure word of prophecy; whereunto ye do well that ye take heed, as unto a light that shineth in a dark place, until the day dawn, and the day star arise in your hearts: Knowing this first, that no prophecy of the scripture is of any private interpretation. For the prophecy came not in old time by the will of man: but holy men of God spake as they were moved by the Holy Ghost."

Testimony of Paul

In my text, the Apostle Paul testifies to the inspiration of the Scripture: *"All scripture is given by inspiration."* The word *inspiration* is a combination of two Greek words. The first is *theos*, from which we get the word *God. Theology* also comes from *theos.* The second is *pneuma*, from which we get the word *pneumonia*, the disease of the breath box, of the lungs. *Theos* and *pneuma*—put these two words together, and in English we have *inspiration.* In the true rendering, all Scripture is "God-breathed." We reject any partial inspiration.

The modernists and liberals will say, "We believe the Bible *contains* the Word of God. A portion of it truly must be inspired, but not all of it."

We reject any such idea. To begin with, if we accept such a nonsensical, illogical approach to the Scripture, who is going to say which verse, which chapter, which book is inspired and which is not?

We believe in the verbal inspiration of the Scripture. The word that is written expresses what God meant for it to say. God said what He meant, and God meant what He said. We believe further in the plenary inspiration—that is, the whole book. We believe the Bible is inspired in its entirety—book by book, chapter by chapter, line by line, verse by verse, word by word, syllable by syllable. I am of this persuasion: If we accept any of the Bible as the holy, infallible, inspired Scriptures, we ought to accept all of it. And the one thing that has marked Baptists in particular is the literal approach we make to the Word of God, believing the Bible is *theospneuma*, "God-breathed," inspired.

The Bible Is Unique

The Bible is a unique Book, and the uniqueness of the Book supports its inspiration. First, it is unique in its *authorship*. God is the Author of the Book. I read in Exodus 24:4, "And Moses wrote all the words of the Lord. . . ." I read in I Thessalonians 2:13 where Paul said,

"For this cause also thank we God without ceasing, because, when ye received the word of God which ye heard of us, ye received it not as the word of men, but as it is in truth, the word of God. . . ."

The Bible is unique in its *authority*. The Bible bears the seal and the mark of divine authority. In Jeremiah 30:2 God said to Jeremiah, "Write thee all the words that I have spoken unto thee in a book." The authority of the Book is divine.

The Bible is unique in its *accuracy*. It is the only Book

that is absolutely, finally, totally accurate.

Sir Nelson Glick, a noted Jewish archaeologist, said, "No archaeological discovery has ever controverted one biblical reference." In other words, in all the digging, in all the unearthings, in all the uncoverings of artifacts and finds all over the biblical world, not one single spade of dirt that has been turned over has ever contradicted one line of Scripture. Not one!

Now the modernists and the liberals have supported archaeologists. They kept hoping they would somewhere, sometime uncover one tablet, one stone that would contradict the Scripture. But in all the history of archaeology, not one stone, not one artifact, not one tablet, not one slate, not one brick has ever been uncovered that has ever contradicted or controverted one single Bible reference. That is amazing. The Bible is unique in its accuracy.

The Bible is unique in its *effect on mankind.* Tell me about another book that can turn the hardest heart of the hardest sinner toward God. There's not a book in all the world! No wonder Paul says in Hebrews 4:12,

"For the word of God is quick, and powerful, and sharper than any twoedged sword, piercing even to the dividing asunder of soul and spirit, and of the joints and marrow, and is a discerner of the thoughts and intents of the heart."

Most of you either read the book or perhaps saw the movie, "Mutiny on the *Bounty.*" The film and the novel are both based on a true story about a British ship called the *Bounty.* The *Bounty* left England in the year 1787 for the South Sea Islands. After ten long months, it finally reached its destination. The crew of the ship spent six months on that island in a particular, specific and designated job they were sent to do. Then they started back to their native country.

Before they were seaborne very long, some of the sailors rebelled. They put Captain Blye and his few faithful men who stood by him out of the ship to face an open sea. The *Bounty* continued on to the Pitcairn Islands with the mutineers aboard.

When they landed, one of the first things they did was to discover a native plant out of which they could distill whiskey. And they did, and that was their ruination. (Let me inject this thought: One of the things ruining America is alcohol.) It was the ruination of this group of sailors that had taken the *Bounty* over, and in process of time, all of them died except one by the name of John Adams.

One day while John Adams was looking through the possessions of one of his late sailor buddies, he found a copy of the Bible. He began to read that Book, and he kept on reading. The Holy Spirit spoke to him, and John Adams was gloriously saved. Then he began to teach the natives the Book of God.

Twenty years went by. Not another man came to that island, but John Adams and a few natives, with one copy of the Bible, started a new colony. It was crime-free. It was disease-free. It was almost trouble-free. After twenty years a ship landed. The passengers were amazed to discover a colony free of crime, free of disease, happy, healthy and prosperous—all because one man was influenced by reading the Book of God.

A Civil War Story

Out of the Civil War comes a story of a captain named Russell Conwell. He had an aid named Johnny Ring. Johnny was a Bible student. Every time he had an opportunity, he slipped his little New Testament out and started reading. One day Conwell said to him, "Johnny, put that foolish Book up. I gave up on that a long time ago. I don't want to see you reading the Bible anymore." But something was in Johnny's heart that drove him to the Book.

In just a few short days Johnny Ring was killed trying to save the life of his captain, Russell Conwell. Conwell testified, "The thing that haunted me most of all was seeing Johnny

Ring reading the Bible, and me scolding him for it." Conwell said, "I ran from God. I knew God was dealing with me."

Finally from a hospital bed Russell Conwell trusted Christ as his Saviour. He founded what is now the *Minneapolis Tribune* (then the *Minneapolis Chronicle*). He became a Baptist preacher. He built the Temple Baptist Church in Philadelphia, seating over 4,000 people. And during his ministry, 6,000 people were recorded converts—all because of Johnny Ring's reading the Bible and the influence of the Word of God upon one man.

I say, the Bible is unique because of the effect it has on humanity.

What about the books in the canon of the Scripture? We talk about books that are canonical—that is, within the canon of the sixty-six books—and some that are noncanonical—that is, outside, extra-biblical. How do we know the difference?

I would answer by saying, first, that there was no human editorial plan in the composition of the Scriptures. Now, if a man were going to have a volume like the Bible, with sixty-six separate books written, he would have a number of people planning and programming—you on this area, you write in this, you write about this, and you write over here. Not so the Bible.

Nobody, for example, set Matthew down and said, "Now, Matthew, I want you to write your Gospel and portray Christ as a King." Nobody said to Mark, "When you write, portray Him as a servant." Nobody said to Luke, "When you write, portray Him as a man." Nobody said to John, "When you write, portray Him as God." There was no editorial plan—except in the mind of God. All Scripture is given by inspiration of God. It was God who led Matthew to write as he wrote and Mark to write as he wrote and all the other writers of the New Testament to write as they wrote.

As to the Old Testament, we know there are thirty-nine books. The original Jewish classification was twenty-four, equivalent to our thirty-nine. Each of the Old Testament books was accepted as the Word of God by the people to whom it was written. By that I mean, no one ever questioned whether or not the prophecy of Jeremiah in Jeremiah's day was the written Word of God. They accepted it. And so it was with all thirty-nine books of the Old Testament. Josephus declares that no sacred writings were composed after the days of King Artaxerxes, which would be about 424 B.C.— 424 years before Christ. That means the last book included in the canon of the Old Testament was the book we know as Malachi. After that, as far as Old Testament writings are concerned, no sacred books were written.

As to the New Testament, there are twenty-seven books. Let me read you one of the best commentaries on the inspiration of the Scripture in all the Bible, II Peter 3:15,16:

"And account that the longsuffering of our Lord is salvation; even as our beloved brother Paul also according to the wisdom given unto him hath written unto you; As also in all his epistles, speaking in them of these things; in which are some things hard to be understood, which they that are unlearned and unstable wrest, as they do also the other scriptures, unto their own destruction."

Peter was referring to the Old Testament when he said the "other scriptures." Hundreds of times in the New Testament, the Old Testament is quoted. Paul gives us fourteen of the twenty-seven books in the New Testament. Peter gives us two. What Peter is saying is that the books Paul and the other writers of the Bible wrote are the Scriptures. In the same manner in which the Old Testament is inspired, the New Testament is also inspired. So this is Peter's approval of the acceptance of the writing of Paul. All fourteen books of the New Testament written by Paul are in the canon of the New Testament.

Requirements of Inspiration

Four requirements must be met if a book is accepted as

being inspired: (1) The book either had to be written by an apostle or confirmed by an apostle—that is, its authorship had to be confirmed; (2) It had to enjoy universal acceptance since the days of the apostles; (3) It had to have been read in all the churches; (4) It had to be recognized by the church fathers as being inspired.

After careful and prayerful consideration of all the books that were having claim of being holy, sacred and inspired writings, only twenty-seven met all four of these requirements, and they are the books in the New Testament, beginning with Matthew and going through the Revelation.

But somebody asks, "What about the apocrypha?" *Apocrypha* means "hidden" or "of spurious content"; and authorship, unknown and uncertain. Fourteen books are called the apocrypha. They were written between the closing of the Old Testament, after Malachi, and the opening of the New Testament, before Matthew. These fourteen books contain Jewish history and customs. The Jews themselves never considered them as sacred writings. Not one Jewish historian nor Jewish philosopher ever considered them as sacred writings. Not one Jewish historian nor Jewish philosopher ever considered a single book of their own—the books of the apocrypha—as being inspired writings.

Not one of the fourteen books of the apocrypha is quoted one single time in the New Testament. It was only four hundred years ago that eleven out of the fourteen books of the apocrypha were included in the Catholic Bible at the Council of Trent in the year 1546 A.D.

So we are well within bounds to say that the books of the apocrypha, the hidden books written between Malachi and Matthew, are non-canonical, outside the realm of inspiration, and do not belong in our Bible.

Looking at the Bible

Look at the Bible for a moment. It is a library of divine truth written by God, interpreted by the Holy Spirit and having as its subject matter the Lord Jesus Christ. The Bible contains history, prophecy, law, literature, drama, poetry, music, philosophy, science, theology, biology, ethnology and all other areas of human knowledge.

The Bible was written over a period of 1600 years—from about 1500 B.C. to 100 A.D. It was written by forty different writers. Kings wrote it. Paupers, priests, preachers, prophets and at least one doctor, the physician Luke, had a part in writing it.

There are sixty-six books in the Bible. They came to us originally in two languages. The Old Testament was written (with the exception of two or three passages in Ezra, Daniel and Jeremiah) in Hebrew. The entire New Testament, without exception, was written in Greek.

The Bible was written from many countries spread over at least two continents. It was written in prisons, in palaces, in caves, on mountains, on the oceans, in the valleys, on the hilltops, on the islands and in other places all over those two continents. God brought forty people together in their writing over 1600 years; yet the Bible is one complete, total library of divine truth. There is not one single error. We believe this Book is inspired!

When they copied the books, the Hebrew scholars were very careful. The first thing they would do was count every Hebrew letter in the Old Testament in that book, then transcribe it—that is, copy it. Then after copying a book, they would go back and count the letters again. If they missed one letter, they would tear it up and go back and start all over again. How meticulous they were! It is inspired by God through holy men of old as they, being moved upon by the Holy Spirit, wrote.

Beloved, the Bible doesn't need to be rewritten. It needs to be reread.

Has any other book stood the test of time that the Bible has stood? For example, do you suppose you could find sixty-six medical journals, written over a period of 1600 years by forty different doctors, and ever treat a man for his disease? No, you could not. It is almost impossible to get two doctors to agree on treatments for the same patient with the same ailment in the same day. You could never get sixty-six medical journals, composed over 1600 years by forty different doctors, to agree on anything.

Suppose you took sixty-six science journals and did the same. A science book, written in 1962, is now obsolete. Put it away and forget it. You would have the same results as with the medical journals—no agreement. Fifty million pages of science come off the press every year, and one by one they are becoming obsolete. The Bible is the only Book that has stood the test of time, having one central message—salvation by the grace of God through Jesus Christ.

Inspiration and Prophecy

One sure evidence of the inspiration of the Scripture is fulfilled prophecy. Let me share with you an experiment some students made in the Pasadena City College in Pasadena, California, a few years ago.

After applying the laws of probability to the fulfillment of eight Old Testament prophecies, here is what they concluded!

As to the birth of Christ, as prophesied in Micah 5:2, there would be only one chance in 280,000 that it would ever come to pass.

As to the prophecy, that a messenger named John would go before Him and announce His birth, as prophesied in Malachi 3:1, the chances are one in one thousand that this would ever happen.

As to the prophecy that He would make His triumphant entry into the city of Jerusalem riding on a colt, as prophesied in Zechariah 9:9, there is only one chance in ten thousand that this would ever happen according to the laws of probability.

That He would be betrayed by a friend, as prophesied

in Zechariah 13:6: there is one chance in a thousand.

That His betrayer would receive thirty pieces of silver, as recorded in Zechariah 11:12: there is only one chance in ten thousand that this would ever happen according to the laws of probability.

That the silver that was paid for Him would be thrown to the potter, as prophesied in Zechariah 11:13: there is one chance in 100,000 that it would ever come to pass.

The prophecy that He would offer no defense when He was accused, as prophesied in Isaiah 53:7: there is one chance in 10,000 that this prophecy would ever come to pass.

The prophecy that He would die by crucifixion, as prophesied in Psalm 22:6: there is only one chance in ten thousand that this prophecy would ever come true.

Based on these estimates, the class figured that the chance of all eight prophecies being fulfilled by one person would be the equivalent of 280,000 times 1,000, times 10,000, times 1,000, times 10,000, times 100,000, times 10,000, times 10,000. This is an astronomical figure that says the odds are against these prophecies ever being fulfilled. But the New Testament tells us that every single one of them was fulfilled just like it was prophesied, right down to the minutest detail.

Where was Jesus born? In Bethlehem, just like Micah said. How did He die? By crucifixion on the cross, just like Isaiah said He would. How much was paid for Him? Thirty pieces of silver, just like Zechariah said. How did He ride into the city of Jerusalem in His triumphal entry? On a colt, just like Zechariah said He would. All these prophecies going against all the odds of the laws of probability came to pass in the Person of Jesus Christ.

Let's look momentarily at one other example, the book of Isaiah. Isaiah lived and prophesied in the eighth century before Christ. His ministry was carried on from about 740 to 700 B.C., a period of forty years, and 740 years before Christ. In Isaiah 45:1, Isaiah called a man by name who had not yet been born—Cyrus. Cyrus was referred to by name by Isaiah 150 years before Cyrus was born. He designated him as the ruler of the Medo-Persian Empire, a place no one had ever heard of. But in 550 B.C., Cyrus came on the scene and became the great head of the Medo-Persian Empire. Amazing! Fantastic! One hundred fifty years before he was born Isaiah called him by name.

In the prophecy of Isaiah (7:14), we have the virgin birth of Christ; in 9:6,7, His deity; in 11:1, His ancestors; in 42:6, His ministry; and in chapter 53, His death. All of these were prophesied over seven hundred years before Christ was born, yet every one of them came to pass just like Isaiah said.

One of the most attacked books in the Bible is Deuteronomy. The modern, liberal critics have designated five different authors for Deuteronomy. Jesus quoted from it many times. He referred to the first five books as the law of Moses, thereby ascribing Mosaic authorship to that book. Deuteronomy was written about 1400 B.C., that is, fourteen hundred years before Christ. In Deuteronomy 4:27, by inspiration of the Holy Spirit, Moses said, "God will drive you out of your land and scatter you among all the nations." Seven hundred years later, in 722 B.C., that prophecy was partially fulfilled when the Assyrians came and took the northern kingdom of Israel, the ten tribes, into captivity. Its complete fulfillment came in the year 70 A.D. when the Romans, under Titus, marched against Jerusalem and scattered the Jews, during which time one million were killed. Titus took a plow and plowed up the city of Jerusalem just like the Old Testament prophet said he would. And from 70 A.D. (just forty years after Christ) until 1948, the Jews had no homeland. They became a state in 1948, as history records. In 1967, during the Six-day War, they took the sight upon which the Temple was built. The Word of God has been accurately fulfilled.

Peter sums up the finality and accuracy of the Bible in I Peter 1:23-25:

"Being born again, not of corruptible seed, but of incorruptible, by the word of God, which liveth and abideth for ever. For all flesh is as grass, and all the glory of man as the flower of the grass. The grass withereth, and the flower thereof falleth away: But the word of the Lord endureth for ever."

The Bible is like tritium. Tritium is a chemical tracer used in scientific detective work. For example, an oil company will use tritium to put in an oil well they have drilled at one point in order that it will be traced to other areas, so when the other wells start pumping, they will know where it came from. I understand tritium can be broken down a million, million, million times, and you can still detect it. That is just like the Bible. You can cut it up, chew it up, spit it out, isolate it, break it down and tear it apart, and still detect that it is the Word of God—the Bible.

In the year 1490 Gutenberg invented the first movable press—that is, a printing press with movable type, and the Bible was printed in 1490 for the first time in its entirety. Today a copy of that original is in the Library of Congress and valued at more than one million dollars.

You have heard the name Voltaire mentioned a number of times, even from this pulpit. Voltaire was an eighteenth-century agnostic, philosopher, writer and poet, but an infidel—an unbeliever. Voltaire said, "One hundred years from now there will be no Bibles." Ironically, the very room where he spoke that is a distribution center for Bibles to be sent all over the world.

On December 24, 1933, they gathered all of Voltaire's works together for a sale. Remember, he was a noted author, poet, philosopher and great scientist. Do you know what his works sold for totally? Eleven cents! (Why, Hitler's car sold for $153,000 yesterday, and Voltaire's works sold for eleven cents!) Yet he said there would not be a Bible around anywhere in one hundred years.

On the same day, December 24, 1933, one manuscript of

the Bible, the Codex Sinaiticus, was purchased by the Russian government from the British government for $500,000. One manuscript! How many manuscripts are there? Over four thousand Greek manuscripts of the New Testament. One manuscript sold for $500,000 the same day Voltaire's works sold for eleven cents!

We believe the Bible is the inspired, infallible, inerrant, indestructible, indisputable, unadulterated, unmistakable, unchanging and unchangeable Word of the living God. This is our premise. Upon this we stand. Here we stand with all force declaring to the world that we believe in the inspiration of the Scriptures.

The Bible at Work

A missionary, Bishop Oldham, went to India. He gathered about him every night a group of natives who had never heard the name of Jesus, who had never heard about a Bible and who had never read one single line in a Bible. Night after night he gathered these men around him. He always left his Bible in his tent and talked extemporaneously. He talked to them about God, about Christ, about the Bible.

One night after he had spent a long time in a lengthy discussion, the leader, an old man with a long, white, flowing beard, said to him, "Young man, the words you have spoken to us tonight are words of wisdom. You are young and I am old, and I know these are words of wisdom. Where did you learn them?"

The missionary answered, "I learned them from a Book."

"You mean to tell me all you have taught us tonight is written in a Book?"

"Yes, I mean to tell you exactly that. It's all written in a Book."

The old man said, "Tell me, young man, is that Book in my language?"

The missionary answered, "Yes, as a matter of fact, it is in your language."

The old man said, "Young man, please bring me that Book."

The missionary went back to his tent and hurriedly came back with two copies of the Bible in their native tongue. He handed one to the old man, the leader, and kept one.

The old man said again, "Did you say that the words you have spoken tonight are found in this Book?"

"Yes, they are found in this Book."

"How long has this Book been written?"

"Oh, for thousands of years."

"Have your people had this Book all that time?"

"Why, yes; my people have had this Book for hundreds of years."

The old man, with trembling voice and tears trickling down his cheeks, said, "Young man, if all those words you have spoken are written in this Book and my family and my friends have died without it, why haven't you brought me this Book before?"

I wonder if that could not be echoed around the world on every continent and out of every tribe of humankind. Men are saying, "Why doesn't somebody bring me the Book?" Over two thousand languages and not one verse of Scripture. Do we really believe in the inspiration of the Scripture? Do we really believe it is God's Book? If we do, let us start sharing it with somebody else. The words in this Book are sufficient to make one wise unto salvation.

2

THE BIBLE

and Creation

"In the beginning God created the heaven and the earth."— Gen. 1:1.

In dealing with creation, we have two basic choices: to believe the fables of men or to believe the fiat—that is, the Word of God. We have long since made our choice. The poet worded it like this:

> **O happy day that fixed my choice**
> **On Thee, my Saviour and my God!**
> **Well may this glowing heart rejoice**
> **And tell its raptures all abroad.**
>
> **Happy day, happy day,**
>   **When Jesus washed my sins away!**
> **He taught me how to watch and pray,**
>   **And live rejoicing ev'ry day;**
> **Happy day, happy day,**
>   **When Jesus washed my sins away!**

I cannot conceive of anybody knowing the Lord Jesus Christ as his personal Saviour who would deny the authenticity of the Genesis account of creation. Man has written endless volumes on the creation of the heavens and the earth; God said it all in seven words. In the Hebrew, Genesis 1:1 contains only seven words. This is remarkable, because the number seven becomes the number of divine completion.

This universe, this earth, this world, is not operated by chance. God set into motion everything necessary for the operation of the great system of the universe. There are numbers, there are numerics in everything. In art, in science, in the philosophical area of life, numbers fit into every area of man's existence. And there is no number like the number seven. Three is the heavenly number. It generally speaks of the thrice Holy God: the Father, the Son and the Holy Spirit. Four is earth's number. We speak, for example, of the directions of the points of the compass—north, south, east, west. Bring them together, and we have the number seven. It is no accident that the first verse of the Bible contains only seven words in the Hebrew in which it was written.

We believe the Genesis account of creation. "In the beginning God created the heaven and the earth." The question might arise, "How can we rely on what Moses wrote since these things happened uncounted, unnamed, unnumbered, unmeasured years before Moses lived?" The answer: we accept it and rely upon it by authority of the inspiration of the Word of God. All Scripture is given by inspiration of God. Holy men of old wrote as they were moved or carried along by the Holy Spirit.

Liberalism and infidelity deny the Mosaic authorship of the Pentateuch: Genesis, Exodus, Leviticus, Numbers, Deuteronomy. The liberals and the infidels are twin sons of Satan, and we do not believe the sons of the Devil, but the Son of God.

And in Mark 12:26 Jesus puts His approval and sanction

upon the Mosaic authorship of the Pentateuch when He asks the question, "Have ye not read in the book of Moses. . .?" Every Jew alive knows that the book of Moses is the Pentateuch—the first five books of the Bible. Jesus was speaking to a Jewish audience when He said, "Have ye not read in the book of Moses. . .?" We, then, stand firmly, uncompromisingly, unmovably upon the Genesis account of creation.

The critics vow that there was no writing at the time of Moses. The archaeologists have a different story. In the year 1905 near Mt. Sinai where Moses received the tablets of the law from God, stones were uncovered that contained an alphabet dating back to the year 1800 B.C. Moses lived in 1400 B.C. Therefore, according to those who uncovered these stones by archaeology in 1905, these stones tell us that there was writing 400 years before Moses.

Further, since 1940, in Ur of the Chaldees, the city where Abraham lived, they have uncovered libraries, schools, universities, stones and tablets that contain writings and an alphabet dating back before Abraham.

But suppose we stopped at Abraham's day. Abraham lived two thousand years B.C. Moses lived 1,400 years B.C.; so there was writing at least 600 years before Moses. In recent years the spade of the archaeologist has uncovered writings that date as early as 3,600 B.C. If Moses lived 1,400 B.C. and there was writing 3,600 B.C., there was writing at least 2,200 years before Moses.

I repeat, we do not believe the liberals and infidels; we believe the Son of God and the Word of God.

Book of Beginnings

The book of Genesis is the book of beginnings. The beginning of every human institution is in the book of Genesis. Genesis means "origin, beginning," and there it all began. In Genesis 1:1 we have basically the assumption of the existence of God and, in the second place, the creation of the heaven and the earth. There is no definition given of God, but who can define the Almighty? There is no declaration of a date, but who can put a date on the Infinite One?

Beloved, when we deal with God, we lay aside our almanacs; we cover up our calendars. God is without measure. I read in Romans 11:33-36:

"O the depth of the riches both of the wisdom and knowledge of God! how unsearchable are his judgments, and his ways past finding out! For who hath known the mind of the Lord? or who hath been his counsellor? Or who hath first given to him, and it shall be recompensed unto him again? For of him, and through him, and to him, are all things: to whom be glory for ever. Amen."

How could we begin to measure God? Peter, in II Peter 3:8, says,

"Beloved, be not ignorant of this one thing, that one day is with the Lord as a thousand years, and a thousand years as one day."

There is no attempt in the Bible to prove the existence of God. The Bible is not a book of proofs; it is a Book of divine revelation. Now there are—and you know them—philosophical arguments that make some attempt to prove that God exists: the *cosmological* argument; the *ontological* argument; and the *teleological* argument.

We do not need a philosophical argument to prove to us that God exists any more than we need astronomy to tell us the sun is shining. We feel its rays. We do not need philosophical arguments to tell us that God exists any more than we would need to memorize by heart the Hippocratic Oath to know that doctors exist. We need simply faith in the inspired and infallible Word of God.

The most sublime statement in human language is this: "In the beginning God . . . ." It brings us into the majestic presence of the Almighty. It kindles the spark that lights all of divine revelation. If you believe these first four words in the Bible—"In the beginning God"—you will have no problem with any other part of the Scripture. These are the most staggering words ever spoken or penned. And to me, the most exciting, most profound, most astonishing, most amazing and most staggering thing about Genesis 1:1 is that it tells us that God IS, and all is well.

The first page of the Bible bears a striking resemblance to the last page, and God is on both. Jesus said, "I am Alpha and Omega, the beginning and the end." I repeat, God IS, and all is well. All is blessing, love, light and rest because God IS. In Hebrews 11:6 we read, ". . . he that cometh to God must believe that he is, and that he is a rewarder of them that diligently seek him."

Heresies Refuted

Consider the heresies refuted in Genesis 1:1: "In the beginning God created the heaven and the earth."

Atheism is refuted. Atheism denies the existence of God. I lay over against that Genesis 1:1, "In the beginning God . . . ."

Deism is refuted. Deism does not deny the existence of God, but Deism denies that God reveals Himself to man. I put over against that Hebrews, chapter 1, "God, who at sundry times and in divers manners spake in time past unto the fathers by the prophets, Hath in these last days spoken unto us by his Son." Deism is refuted.

Agnosticism is refuted. An agnostic says, "We can't know whether there is a God." I ask the agnostic, "How can there be a design without a designer? How can there be a product without a producer? And how can there be a creation without a Creator?"

Materialism is refuted. Those who hold a philosophical system of materialism say that all matter is eternal, that there was never a time when matter did not exist, and that everything is material. Nothing spiritual in all the universe, all is material. Genesis 1:1 says, "In the beginning . . .," and God is not material.

Pantheism is refuted. The pantheists say that the universe is God and God is the universe. Everything is one substance. But the Bible says, "In the beginning God . . ."—one separate Being—"created the heaven and the earth." Something different. They are not the same.

Rationalism is refuted. Rationalism says that nothing exists beyond reason. Beloved, where our human reasoning ends, faith begins—Hebrews 11:3: "Through faith we understand that the worlds were framed by the word of God."

Fatalism is refuted. Fatalism says everything is by chance. You are by chance. This building is by chance. The tree out on the parking lot is by chance. The river that runs to the ocean is by chance. The stars that light the sky at night are by chance. The sun is by chance. The moon is by chance. The cow is by chance. The dog is by chance. The bird is by chance.

It makes just as much sense to say that this designed, planned, universal system of ours is by chance as to say that Webster's unabridged dictionary is the result of an explosion in a print shop. This world is *not* by chance, but by creation. And it is not run by chance, but by laws of God that cannot and must not change; for God says: "I the Lord God change not." I read in Isaiah 44:6, "I am the first, and I am the last; and beside me there is no God."

Polytheism, the belief in many gods, is refuted. There is but *one* God. "Hear, O Israel, the Lord thy God is one." The creation is revealed for us—heaven and earth in Genesis 1:1—we believe to be the work of God.

In this message we deal with three basic questions.

1. When Was Creation?

The words, "In the beginning," denote a time without a date. The time of the creation cannot be ascertained or even assumed. We reckon chronology from the creation of man, not from the creation of the earth. There is no way we can know how old this earth is. The safest, soundest and most sensible approach to the question of how old creation is, is this: accept the fact that the time element is known only by God. God never intended or expected us to know. If He had, I believe Genesis 1:1 might have read like this: "Five hundred million years before the flood, God created the heaven and the earth." Then we could go back and say that the Flood was about 2,400 B.C.; therefore, the earth was created five hundred million two thousand four hundred years before Christ. Nonsense! Genesis 1:1 does not read, 500 million or 5 billion years ago God created the heaven and the earth. Genesis simply says, "In the beginning. . . ." In the dateless past, God created the heaven and the earth.

It seems that creation was progressive. First, matter was created—the heaven and the earth as declared in Genesis 1:1. Then the world of nature and man were created—Genesis 1:2-27. How long between the creation of the earth and man? No one can say with absolute certainty or assurance. There are those who hold to the Gap Theory, that somewhere between Genesis 1:1 and Genesis 1:2 there was a cataclysmic judgment, perhaps the fall of Satan out of Heaven. You remember that Jesus said, "I beheld Satan as lightning fall from heaven" (Luke 10:18). I would not stand and say to you dogmatically that there is a gap between Genesis 1:1 and Genesis 1:2. Perhaps there is. I do not believe anyone really knows for sure. I repeat, the systems of matter, heaven and earth were created as recorded in Genesis 1:1, and then afterwards, the world of nature and mankind.

The question often arises, "Were the six days of creation, recorded in Genesis 1:2-27, 24-hour days, the solar days as we know them?" (More accurately, a day is 23 hours, 56 minutes and 4 seconds.) Were they 24-hour days? I believe they were. I believe the tenor of Scripture would indicate that.

For example, in Exodus 20, when God is laying out the plan and program for man, we read that in six days God created the heaven and earth and on the seventh day He rested. Then God gives a pattern of man's labor and work: six days of work, one day of rest. Some people have the thing in reverse!

The word *day* in the Hebrew is *yom*. It appears in the Old Testament no less than 1,480 times. It is translated in our English version by fifty-six different words. *Day* could mean a solar day—twenty-four hours. It could mean an extended, indefinite period of time, like a thousand years. It could mean an uncounted, unmeasured period of time. "In that day" appears many times in the Scriptures. Eleven hundred and eighty-one times *yom* is translated "day," probably meaning a 24-hour solar day. Sixty-seven times it's translated "time." Thirty times it's translated "today." Eighteen times it's translated "forever." Ten times it's translated "continually." Six times it's translated "age." Four times it's translated "life." Twice it's translated "perpetually."

We cannot say dogmatically what period of time existed between the creation of heaven and earth and the creation of man, nor whether those six days were solar days. However, I personally believe that they were.

2. What Was Created?

"The heaven and the earth." Now remember, the Old Testament was written in Hebrew, and it was written expressly in its original for Hebrew thinkers. "In the beginning God created the heaven . . . ." The same word in the Hebrew for "heaven" is used for universe. And the universe is absolutely measureless. Universe is the whole universal system, including the earth and all the other planets, all of the other galaxies, and all of the other stars.

Did you know, for example, that our earth is in a galaxy that is in the midst of nineteen other galaxies? And that in our galaxy, scientists tell us there may be billions and billions of stars never yet seen? And that there might be as many as one billion galaxies? Now, if there are a billion galaxies and every galaxy has at least a billion stars, no wonder Jeremiah 33:22 says that "the host of heaven [universe in Hebrew] cannot be numbered." The vast, trackless, measureless universal system cannot be measured.

God created the heaven, the universe—whatever that includes—and there are multiplied millions of galaxies that we know nothing of.

But, then, Genesis 1:1 tells us that God created the earth. It all narrows down from Genesis 1:2 through the rest of the Bible to *one race* in *one age* on *one planet*. Who would venture a guess what might be elsewhere? But the Bible is written for one race, in one age, on one planet, the earth. Beyond this, we do not know, nor are we wise to speculate what might be elsewhere. In the beginning God created the universe, the trackless, measureless reaches of space, and the earth, the planet upon which mankind was placed.

3. How Did God Create?

What process was used? There are no details on how God created. A little later on in a message, "The Bible and Science," I relate some of the fantastic ideas of man as to how this thing came about. Let me mention just one here.

Some say there was a mass of gases, the gases cooled off, and a chunk went this way, and they called it the earth. A chunk went that way, and they called it Mars. A chunk went that way, and they called it something else. But the Bible says, "God created . . . ." It is not for us to know the depth of the wisdom of God, but to believe what God says. The marvel of grace is that we do not have to understand; we're only asked to believe. The sublimity and profundity of creation is seen in its absolute simplicity—"In the beginning God . . . ."

Create in Hebrew is *para*, meaning to bring into existence something out of nothing. And that's precisely what God did. Man cannot do it. The word *made* is *asah*. Man can make and manufacture, but man cannot create. In the science of thermodynamics, there are two basic laws: Matter can neither be created nor destroyed, and all systems that now exist are decaying. What does this mean? That man cannot create nor destroy that which has been created. And here's something to think about. I believe it further indicates that this universe (whatever that entails, whatever that involves, whatever that includes) and this earth are both decaying in favor of a new heaven and a new earth that John talks about in the Revelation: "And I saw a new heaven and a new earth: for the first heaven and the first earth were passed away." God the Father is the Architect. God the Son is the Builder. "All things were made by him; and without him was not any thing made that was made" (John 1:3). And God the Holy Spirit is the Beautifier. It's that simple. We must accept it by faith.

Did you ever wonder why God didn't give us any details on the creation? Perhaps because in His infinite wisdom He knew that we, in our finite wisdom, could never understand or comprehend the glory of His creative work. One day we shall see clearly the marvels of creation. Who knows? We might take a billion-year trip and visit all the galaxies. Then we'll know more how to say with the psalmist:

"When I consider thy heavens, the work of thy fingers, the moon and the stars, which thou hast ordained," I ask myself the question, *"What is man, that thou art mindful of him? and the son of man, that thou visitest him?"*

If we take a billion-year trip, we will be gone only a few days. There are no clocks in Heaven, no calendars in the Glory world. And we won't have to worry about the ultraviolet rays because in that day when we are like Him, we shall be brighter than the sun.

On the Mount of Transfiguration stood Peter, James, John and the Son of God glorified. The best way they could describe it was to compare His glory to the sun because the brightest thing they had ever seen was the noonday sun.

When Matthew recorded it, he said His radiance and His beauty and His majesty and His glory were brighter than the noonday sun. John declares:

"Beloved, now are we the sons of God, and it doth not yet appear what we shall be: but we know that, when he shall appear, we shall be like him; for we shall see him as he is. And every man that hath this hope in him purifieth himself, even as he is pure."—I John 3:2,3.

We are one day going to be just as pure as Christ because we are going to be just like Him. Ah, won't that be something! Then we won't have to ask, "What does He mean by cosmological?" "What does He mean by teleological?" In that day we shall have all the answers and all the solutions. I praise God that we have the blessed hope that one day it will be our joy to be like Him. Then all the mystery of the creation will be unfolded, and we'll have all knowledge, all wisdom and all understanding.

A few days before Christmas, I was visiting with Mrs. Susie Lawrence, a dear and precious saint of God, a woman of great faith. While talking with her, I said, "Well, Mrs. Lawrence, it was a happy day when you came back home, wasn't it?" (She had spent many days in the hospital.) She replied, "Yes, Brother Barber, it was. But it's going to be a happier day when we go Home to Heaven!"

It's in the Book, and we believe the Book.

"In the beginning God created the heaven and the earth."

3

THE BIBLE

and Evolution
(Part 1)

"**A**nd God said, Let us make man in our image, after our likeness: and let them have dominion over the fish of the sea, and over the fowl of the air, and over the cattle, and over all the earth, and over every creeping thing that creepeth upon the earth. So God created man in his own image, in the image of God created he him; male and female created he them. And God blessed them, and God said unto them, Be fruitful, and multiply, and replenish the earth, and subdue it: and have dominion over the fish of the sea, and over the fowl of the air, and over every living thing that moveth upon the earth."—Gen. 1:26-28.

"And the Lord God formed man of the dust of the ground, and breathed into his nostrils the breath of life; and man *became a living soul."*—Gen. 2:7.

I have read to you from the Genesis account of the creation of man. Only God creates. We believe the Word of God. And what God has said about the creation of mankind, we question not. The creation of man was the last and highest stage in the process of creation. All that God had created before was in preparation for God's masterpiece. The creation of man was the zenith, the masterpiece in God's creation.

Man is the only being created in the image of God. This means, among other things, that man possesses the powers of wisdom and reasoning. Not one single species of the lower animal kingdom possesses the power of wisdom and reasoning. It means that man possesses a conscience. Not one species of the lower animal kingdom possesses a conscience. It means that man possesses dignity of presence. It means that man possesses freedom of choice. Not a species in the lower animal kingdom possesses the freedom of choice. Man is a triune being—three parts: body, soul and spirit. Not a species in all the lower animal kingdom possesses these three. Man is far above any species of the lower animal kingdom.

What Meaneth These Words?

In the beginning of the message, we do well to establish the definition of at least four terms. First—**fact.** Webster says a fact is a thing that has actually happened or is true. The second word—**hypothesis.** Webster says an hypothesis is a theory imagined or assumed to account for what is not understood—in other words, something that has not been proved—if you please, an intelligent guess, a scientific assumption. Three—**theory.** A theory is a mere hypothesis, a guess, a conjecture—so says Webster. Fourth—**evolution,** which means the development of a higher and more complex life from a lower and less complex life.

Evolution—Atheistic and Theistic

In the area of evolution, we would think primarily of two segments or two divisions—atheistic evolution and theistic evolution. *Theistic,* from which both of those words come, is from the root word *theos* which means God. We get our word *theology* from it—the study of the doctrine of God.

To say that one is an atheist means that he does not believe in God. He rules out the possibility of the existence of God. To say that one is theistic in his approach to evolution means that he would accept, entertain and embrace the fact that God lives and indeed created, but not necessarily as the Bible says. The theistic evolutionist says that God may have used a lesser, lower, less complex form of life, out of which He would develop over a period of many myriads of years a higher form of living. Personally, I think it preposterous to teach a theory as a fact.

Let us theorize for a moment. Suppose I say to you, "I have a theory. I believe that, if you put a gram of silver in a bowl of acid, you will sooner or later have a silver dollar." That is a theory. It is unfounded. It is untrue. It is only a guess. It is not even an intelligent guess, because nobody has ever proven that you could put a gram of silver in a bowl of acid and come out with a silver dollar.

I theorize a bit further. Suppose I say to you, "I'll put this watch in the closet. I'll wait and wait and wait; then finally this watch will become a grandfather clock." This is precisely what the evolutionists are doing. They are theorizing.

There is not one word of proof in the theory of evolution. The real issue in evolution opposed to the Bible account of creation is not *how* and *when* did life begin; the real issue is this, particularly in atheistic evolution: "Is God true? And is His Word trustworthy?"

Many liberal and modern theologians are expounding this theistic evolution idea. There are reasons why I cannot. First, it is not biologically sound nor true; second, it does not answer the deep, difficult questions of life.

For example: theistic evolutionists say that out there some-where in the atmosphere there were gases; and my first ques-tion is, "Where did the atmosphere come from?" I get the answer from the Bible, not through theistic evolution.

Out there in the atmosphere where the gases were, a bolt of lightning struck the gases and formed some chemical par-ticle that was heavier than the gases, heavier than air, so it fell into the ocean. I want to know where the ocean came from. There formed some amino acids. I want to know where the acids came from. And then there might have been a fish and a reptile, then a mammal. I want to know where all these came from. Theistic evolution has never answered those questions.

Atheistic evolution attacks God, the Bible, Christ, Christi-anity and the Christian. Either evolution is right and the Bible is wrong, or the Bible is right and evolution is wrong. Atheistic evolution attacks the whole plan and program of redemption. It makes a mockery of the cross and incarna-tion of Christ, as well as the process of redemption through faith in His wonderful work upon Calvary's tree. Atheistic evolution declares that life began of itself, apart from God.

Darwin's "Origin of the Species"

The most renowned exponent of evolution was the pro-fessor, Charles Darwin. His most widely circulated book is *The Origin of the Species.* Charles Darwin said on page 523:

> Analogy would lead me to the belief that all animals and plants are descended from some one prototype. All organisms started from a common origin from which low and interme-diate forms both of animals and plants may have been devel-oped. All the organic beings which have ever lived on the earth may be descended from some one primordial form.

Did you notice the words "may be" or "may have been"? In this book, no less than eight hundred times, "Let us assume" or "We may well suppose" appears. I've never, in the Bible story of creation, found one single assumption. Not one single time nor place has God through His inspired writers said, "We may assume" or "Let us suppose."

Evolution in Laymen's Language

In the laymen's language, here is the theory of evolution.

Once upon a time—nobody knows when—at some given place—nobody knows where—a speck of protoplasmic substance—nobody knows what—came into existence—no one knows how—over a period of time—no one knows how long. From that one speck of protoplasm there developed—and no one knows how—all the forms of life in the animal and vegetable world. Or we might state it in one phrase: "From amoeba to man."

To put it plainly and somewhat crudely: Out there somewhere was a mud puddle. An evolutionist doesn't know where the mud came from—just from somewhere out there. For some reason or other, there was water, and in that water was a protozoan, an amoeba, a one-celled animal—a mass of protoplasm. The rays of the sun warmed the water, and life was generated. Then that cell divided and became something more. Finally that one-celled amoeba evolved into a, shall we say, multi-celled being or animal and made its way out of the pool of muddy water. It found it could not go as well on the ground as it went in the water. So through some magic way of exercising itself, it grew a foot. Finally, it grew another foot. Finally, it grew a paw and another paw, then a tail. Then it climbed a tree, then came down, stood up and said, "I am a man."

How ridiculous! I find that much more difficult to believe than the Word of God.

Widely accepted is this theory of evolution in the school systems all over America. I recently read where there is a suit issued in the state of California against the school systems for teaching evolution as a fact. It is *not* a fact. It is nothing more than a scientific guess. If man evolved from that one-celled amoeba, why are there still billions and billions and billions of one-celled amoeba around? Why did just *one* pop out?

When I was in college, they set an instrument before me in biology that they called a microscope. On a little glass plate was a speck of something that I could not see. As I looked at it under the glass, I saw something moving in seven directions. I asked the teacher, "What is that?" She answered, "Why, that is an amoeba." "An amoeba? What is that?" I asked. She explained that it was a mass of protoplasm.

My question to you is: if life began as we know it and, out of that one-celled amoeba, has evolved into the intelligence of man, why do we still have billions of them around? Why haven't they all developed into some higher complex of life?

The Genesis account says that God said, "Let us make man in our image." I have already said that man is a triune being—body, soul and spirit. He is in the moral image and likeness of God. "Let us"—Father, Son and Holy Spirit.

All of us who believe in the Genesis account are called, among other things, **creationists.** We believe in the creation of the heaven and the earth and everything thereupon, by God Himself. Those who believe in the theory of evolution are called **evolutionists.** I'm happy to classify us among that untold, unnamed, unnumbered, uncounted and uncompromising group who have lived and died clinging to our faith in the Word of God that teaches that God made man in His own likeness and in His own image.

To deny the Genesis account of creation is to disbelieve God. And to disbelieve God is to make God a liar. God said He made man. To disbelieve God is to disbelieve Christ. To disbelieve the Genesis account is to disbelieve the Lord Jesus because Jesus believed that God created man. "God made them male and female" (Mark 10:6). If we do not believe the Bible, we cannot believe God. If we do not believe God, we are condemned. "He that believeth is not condemned, but he that believeth not is condemned already." To be condemned is to be forever lost. To be lost is to be separated from God. To be separated from God means that one's name has not been written in the Lamb's book of life. Those whose names have not been written in the Lamb's book of life shall one day be cast into a lake of fire that burneth with fire and brimstone forever and ever and ever. Let God be true and every man a liar.

Three basic questions:

1. By What Process Did Man Come Into Existence?

By a special creative act of God.

"And the Lord God formed man of the dust of the ground, and breathed into his nostrils the breath of life; and man became a living soul."—Gen. 2:7.

God did not make part of a man, then leave the rest to the process of evolution. God made the man whole, complete. God made the man think, talk, act. The first thing Adam did was to name every beast and fowl in the air. This speaks of total intelligence. He was perfect morally, perfect intellectually, perfect spiritually.

Evolution says man has gradually become what he is today. One of their ideas is that on that little mass of protoplasm there was a freckle or a bump or a speck somewhere that was sensitive to light, and after it stayed in the light for perhaps millions of years, that sensitive spot became an eye.

Well, now, who on earth told the eye where to be? Suppose it showed up on the end of your finger. And who said there should be two? The same thing about the ear. A sensitive spot that was receptive to sound waves finally became an ear. Why, who told the ear to be where it was? Suppose it was on the bottom of the foot.

There must be an intelligence behind an intelligent being, an intelligence we call God.

I repeat: God made man whole, complete. The word for *man* in Greek is *anthropos.* We get our word *anthropology* from it. *Anthropos* means "the looking up one." Our ancestors were never down on all fours. They weren't animalistic. They were never one-celled. I believe what the Book says—that God formed man out of the dust of the earth, breathed into him the breath of life, and he became a living soul, in the likeness and image of God.

2. In What Fashion Did God Create Man After His Own Image?

There is not one species, not one example out of one species of all the species of the lower animal kingdom that is made in the likeness and image of God. Can evolution ever prove that God has not always been what He is right now?

My scientific adviser, J. W. Huffman, said to me, "I have a question that the evolutionists have never answered: Has there ever been an animal born without a mother? Evolutionists cannot answer that question. They cannot say that there has ever been an animal born without a mother." Then he came up with this idea: "Where was and who was Eve's mother?"

That's something to think about, isn't it? If man evolved and became what he is now, from a lower complex of life, what about Eve's mother? She had no mother. The Bible says God caused a deep sleep to come upon man; then He performed an operation. Out of man, God made the woman. The one who invented chloroform, used for hundreds of years now in surgery, discovered the principle from the account of the deep sleep that God caused to come upon Adam.

You just can't beat the Book! Every known and unknown area of knowledge is in this Book. This is not a book of science; but when it speaks scientifically, it speaks correctly. God made man in His own image.

3. For What Purpose Did God Make Man?

One, to be the keeper of the earth; two, to be the recipient of His blessings; three, to be the subject of His redemption.

God created man and put him in a perfect environment. Go back and trace the history of mankind. You will discover man is not going up but going down. Man is not getting better but getting worse. Man is not being elevated; he is being de-escalated. Man is not climbing higher; he is sinking lower. God made man a wholesome being, and man sinned against God through willful choice of his own. He broke fellowship with God; then God sent His Son to restore that fellowship and to bring that child back home.

This is what the story of redemption is about. In the final analysis, it is important where you came from, but it's more important where you're going!

4

THE BIBLE

and Evolution

(Part 2)

"**A**nd the Lord God formed man of the dust of the ground, and breathed into his nostrils the breath of life; and man became a living soul."—Gen. 2:7.

Scientists and evolutionists through the years have been baffled by many unanswerable questions. Scientists, for example, thought if they could isolate the atom they could discover the secret of life. So they isolated the atom, only to discover that they must divide or split the atom. They thought if they could split the atom they might prove their scientific theories of how life started and from where it came. So they split the atom, only to discover another unanswerable question: Where did the energy within the atom come from? That is a question the scientists have not, as of yet, been able to answer.

We believe we have the answer within the framework of God's Word, in the very first verse of the Bible, "In the beginning God . . . ."

Unanswerable Questions

We believe that God set in motion every law, every movement, all the momentum of all the system of the universe. Man has come to the point where he has been able to harness a little bit of that power here and harness a little bit of that power there, and to delve into some of the mysteries of life, only to remain baffled as to where life had its beginning.

If they would but turn to the Bible! In several places the Apostle Paul says, "I would not have you to be ignorant, brethren." To the scientists and the evolutionists who doubt and who are baffled by the question, "Where did life come from?" I would say, "Who's the Author of life? Who's the Sustainer of life? Sirs, I would not have you to be ignorant any longer. Look within the framework of God's Word for the answer."

There is not one, I repeat, not **one** area of human knowledge not covered in the Bible. There are questions that the evolutionists cannot answer. The more scientists have researched, the more baffled they have become. In reality, the findings of science have served to disprove the theory of evolution and to give credence to the Genesis account: "In the beginning God created the heaven and the earth." The evolutionists cannot answer: WHO? WHERE? WHAT? WHEN? WHY? or HOW? The entire system of evolution is built upon supposition, not upon fact.

Suppose someone said to you, "Once upon a time there was a grain of sand in the desert. Someone spit upon it, and that resulted in the generation of energy. The energy began to work, and soon the grain of sand became a pebble. Time passed, and the pebble became a brick. Time passed, and the brick became a block. Time passed, and the block became a slab. Time passed, and the slab became a pyramid.

So we have the answer: A pyramid evolved from a grain of sand."

You ask that person, "Who spit on it?" And he answers, "I don't know." "Where?" "I don't know." "When?" "I don't know." "How?" "I don't know." "Why?" "I don't know." "What will be next after the pyramid?" "I don't know."

Would you believe such a supposition as that for a fact? Could you ever believe it as a theory? The evolutionists say that life began somewhere, at some time, at some point, somehow, someway and for some reason; but they don't know how or when or where or what or why or what comes next.

If, on the other hand, the same person said to you, "A man once had an idea. He took sand from the desert. He mixed it with other elements. He made a brick, and from that brick he made a bigger stone. And he made a slab, and he gathered men together, and they put a slab here and a slab there, until finally they had built a pyramid," you could believe that.

What I'm saying is this: Behind every design, there must be a designer. Behind everything created, there must be a creator. And the great God of the universe is the Designer, Architect and the Creator of the heaven and the earth.

I said—and I must repeat for emphasis at this point—the entire system of evolution is built on supposition.

Dr. T. N. Tahmisian, a former member of the Atomic Energy Commission, said: "Scientists who go about teaching that evolution is a fact of life are great con men, and the story they are telling may be the greatest hoax ever. In explaining evolution, we do not have one iota of fact." The word of a scientist: ". . .we do not have one iota of fact."

On the other hand, we believe, according to Genesis 1, that every species living now has always lived. There are no new species. There is not one iota of evidence for any new species having come into existence since the day God created all the animal and vegetable life. In other words, a rose is a rose is a rose. A rose has always been a rose—different varieties for sure, but still a rose. A dog has always been a dog—different breeds, different sizes, long dogs, short dogs, high dogs, low dogs—but dogs just the same. A dog has always been a dog. A cat has always been a cat. A horse has always been a horse. A cow has always been a cow. And God through Adam named every one of them!

Man has always been man. Different colors, different creeds, different cultures, different civilizations, but a man has always been a man. There is no record of any species changing into another species. The law of God has fixed the species so that they will never change. In Genesis 1, we read again and again, "after his kind." Every species that God created reproduced "after his kind." In Genesis we have the story plainly, simply, sublimely told. In keeping with the statement, that no record has ever been discovered of one species changing into another, cows have always produced calves, not puppies. In I Corinthians 15:39 are these words: "All flesh is not the same flesh: but there is one kind of flesh of men, another flesh of beasts, another of fishes, and another of birds." All flesh is not the same flesh. That gives credence to what Moses said in Genesis: "after his kind," not after another. That is one basic question the evolutionists have never answered.

Dr. R. G. Lee, one of the most famed preachers in this country, said on one occasion that he had advertised all over the country that, if anybody anywhere could answer this question, it would for him forever solve the problem of evolution: *"Why is it that everything born in this world has its own clothes except the human body?"*

Think about that for a moment. Everything born has its own clothes. A little chick is hatched, and it goes chick, chick, chicking away in its little feathers. Nobody puts a coat on a chicken. A pig is born, and it goes oink, oink, oink, oinking away with its own covering. A cub is born, and it goes on its way with its beautiful fur, clothed by God Himself.

Evolution cannot answer the question, "Why is everything born with clothes except the human body?"

But the Bible has the answer. In Psalm 104:2 we read: "Who coverest thyself with light as with a garment. . . ." God covereth Himself with garments of light. Man is the only creature created in the likeness and image of God. Thus, does it not naturally follow that God clothed Adam and Eve in garments of light; then when they sinned, they were stripped of their garments, and they saw themselves as naked before each other and before God? God had to clothe them with garments. And God has had to clothe human bodies ever since that time.

Evolutionists cannot answer that question. Evolution says that life began of itself; God says He created life. We believe God. This is an ironic thing and rather paradoxical. The greatest enemy evolutionists have is time. They have made more out of time, saying time has brought this, time has brought that; yet time is their greatest enemy for this reason: Time is destructive, not constructive. There are questions unanswered by the evolutionists but answered forthrightly by the Word of God.

Undeniable Hoaxes

I shall speak of hoaxes that the evolutionists cannot deny.

Hoax number one: **The Nebraska Man.** He has also been called the Western man. In the state of Nebraska in 1922, Harold Cook uncovered the so-called fossil of the Nebraska man, or the Western man. He was reportedly one million years old. Around the world the news went: "Man lived in North America a million years ago."

In the Scopes trial in Dayton, Tennessee, which was a trial concerning evolution, the scientists and anthropologists led by H. H. Newman confronted William Jennings Bryan with all of this evidence that Mr. Cook had found. Mr. Bryan pleaded with the court and with these men to give him more time to study the evidence. They laughed at him. They made a joke of it. But God and time were on Mr. Bryan's side.

When the truth was revealed, the so-called fossil that was found was a tooth—not teeth—a tooth; and from this one tooth a great case for evolution was built. In recent years, a whole skeleton that belonged to the animal to which the tooth belonged was found. What do you suppose that animal turned out to be? A pig! Anthropologists took the tooth of a pig and said, "We have found the secret of the age of man"—out of one tooth of a pig! That's one hoax of anthropology and the evolutionists.

Incidentally, over in Colorado they found another fossil, another tooth, and called it the Colorado man. It turned out to be the tooth of a horse. Anthropologists have put more over on people than any other group in all the world.

Hoax number two: **The Java Man.** He was supposed to have been the most outstanding find that archaeologists had ever uncovered and anthropologists had ever known. In 1891, Dr. Eugene DuBois, a Dutch physician, uncovered in central Java several pieces of bone. One was a piece of a skull, one was a piece of a thigh bone, and there were three teeth. These weren't even all found in the same place, but sixty or seventy-five feet apart, in a dry riverbed. They claim that the Java man lived 750,000 years ago. In his book, *Social Evolution*, Dr. Chapin wrote: "It was fortunate that the most distinctive portions of the human frame should have been preserved because from these specimen we are able to construct the entire being."

This man stood halfway between the anthropoid and the existing man. The authorities violently disagreed on what had been found. (Incidentally, the war that has raged among the evolutionists would make the theological wars look like backyard wrestling matches. They agree on only one thing: that life started of itself apart from God. They disagree violently after that point.) So they argued the case.

Shortly after that discovery, twenty-four of the most imminent scientists in Europe met. Ten said these bones discovered in central Java belonged to an ape. Seven said they belonged to a man. Seven said they belonged to the "missing" link.

In 1926, or about thirty-five years later, another so-called Java man was found, a brother of the first. This time the whole skull was found, and they called this the skull of the missing link.

Well, beloved friends, evolution has many missing links to account for. There has never been found a missing link. Why? Because in reality there is no missing link. In fact, there's not even a chain, so they couldn't have a missing link.

Newspaper headlines went all over the world: "Perfect skull of pre-historic man, the missing link, found." They shouted among themselves and to the whole world, "The Java man has a brother!" What was this so-called missing link skull? It turned out to be the knee bone of an elephant! Another hoax of anthropology. The knee bone of an elephant—and they said this is the Java man!

Hoax number three: **The Piltdown Man.** In the year 1912 over in Piltdown, England, in a gravel pit, some bones were found, part of a skull, piece of a jaw and two teeth. Dr. Charles Dawson brought these to the British museum. The anthropologists looked at them, studied them, then said, "They must be 500,000 years old. This is a tremendous find. What a case for evolution!"

They put these bones in a museum, put pictures in the encyclopedias and in textbooks. The Encyclopedia Britannica said: "The Piltdown man is second only in importance to the Java man." So this renewed interest in evolution all over the world. A great find!

In 1956 an article appeared in *Reader's Digest* entitled "The Great Piltdown Hoax." I quote: "Every important piece proved to be a forgery. The Piltdown man was a fraud from start to finish."

The skull turned out to be the skull of a modern man. They said it was 500,000 years old. The teeth turned out to be in the jawbone of an ape. They had actually filed down the teeth to make it appear an aged bone. Another hoax of anthropologists!

Three hundred replicas of the Piltdown man were placed in museums around the world and heralded as the ancestor of modern man. It is estimated that every year one million people pass through the American Museum of Natural History in New York to see this so-called ancestor of the human race.

A hoax of the anthropologists and nothing but a hoax. Not one grain of fact, not one word of truth. From beginning to end, *Reader's Digest* declared the whole thing a fraud and a forgery.

It appears to me that most of the displays in the museums depicting the development of the human race are merely the imagination of the anthropologists. It appears to me they arbitrarily construct a skeleton, taking a bone from here and a bone from there and putting those in the order that they want them to be in. Then they spray a few chemicals on them, give them some fantastic name, put them behind a glass, then put that off on the public as the truth. Even stranger than that, people believe it!

Anthropologists have put frauds over on people, not only of America but around the world. And people believe them. Isn't that strange! Just pick up a few bones here and a few bones there, wash them down real good, put some chemicals on them, put a name on them, write some fantastic story about them, put them behind a glass; and millions of people walk by and say, "My! Look at that! Five hundred thousand years old! One million years old! This is our ancestor!"

How gullible people are! Just because it has a long name on it that nobody can pronounce, just because it has something mystical about it, just because some anthropologist has signed his name to it, does not make it the truth. We'd best stay with the Book. The Lord God formed man out of the dust of the earth, and man became a living soul. It's a shame, a tragedy, that in textbooks placed in American schools, children are taught this. It is nothing in the world but forgery and a hoax on the part of those who want to support their theory of evolution and try to make out of it a fact.

Uncrossed Bridges

There are some *bridges that the evolutionists have never crossed.*

Dr. O. E. Sandin, a member of the American Association for the Advancement of Science, says, "There are at least twelve bridges that the evolutionists have never crossed." I name them only: 1. The bridge of mathematics. 2. The bridge of articulate speech. 3. The bridge of invention. 4. The bridge of man's body. 5. The bridge of morphology, or the structure of man. 6. The bridge of the resurrection. 7. The bridge of moral character. 8. The bridge of conscience. 9. The bridge of man's spiritual nature. 10. The bridge of man's influence. 11. The bridge of the new birth. 12. The bridge of immortality.

The evolutionists have never crossed these bridges. It appears that there are at least four basic differences in the animal kingdom and the human body:

First, **posture.** The word *anthropos*, from which we get our word *man*, means "the looking up one," the erect one.

Again, the anthropologists have in their own wild and frustrated imagination drawn and produced pictures of creatures of so-called ancestors of the human race, bent over, animal-like, gorilla-like. In some of these museums I've seen some of these. To me, the skeleton of an ape looks like an ape. The skeleton of a man looks like a man. Well, somebody said, "Aren't there striking resemblances?" When both man and ape live on the same planet, when both have to eat, when both have to sleep, why wouldn't there be some resemblances? Both were made by the same God. Don't let their resemblance throw you off the track.

Suppose we said, "Here's a little doghouse, here's a big

doghouse, here's a hut, here's a cottage, here's a house, there's a mansion, yonder's a castle. They all have floors, a roof, walls, and they all resemble." But nobody would believe that one came from the other because there might be some resemblance.

Second, man's **countenance.** Man in his countenance has the light of God shining because he's made in the likeness and image of God.

Third, man's **mind.** Did you ever try to teach geometry to an elephant? Did you ever try to teach astrology to a cat? Did you ever try to teach theology to a mule? Some I know are that hardheaded, but you cannot teach a dumb brute, a beast, an animal these intelligent things.

But go to yonder jungle, find the most primitive man, and you can teach him all three because he is a man, because he has a mind, an intellect and reasoning, and he has the potential to learn.

Fourth is man's **soul.** God breathed into man's nostrils, and man became a living soul. Soul separates man from the animal kingdom.

Two years ago there was discovered in the Philippines a tribe called Tassaday tribe. They are as primitive as any so-called pre-historic man. What on earth are the anthropologists going to do with them? Why haven't they developed and evolved into modern man, so-called as we know?

Down in South America there are people who live in brush. If they have any tools at all, they are very simple tools. In Mexico they live in huts. In some instances, their tools are probably a little bit more complex than those in South America. Here in North America we live in houses. We work with power-driven tools.

Suppose a great ice slide or a great mud slide swept down from the North and covered North America and Mexico and South America. A million years pass. What a case for the anthropologists! Here he was when he was bent over, down there in the brush. Here he was when he had a simple tool.

Then he got up a little bit higher and lived in a hut. Then he became a little more developed and lived in a house and worked with power-driven tools. What a case! What a discovery! What a find! Not so! We're all contemporary. We're living at the same time they're living, only in a different culture and different civilization, with more opportunities of advancement.

We certainly have not evolved from the man down in South America. We're older than some of them, so how could we have evolved from them? No case for evolution here.

I would conclude by saying that evolution is no nearer the fact and truth than it ever was. But the Bible, this infallible, inspired Word of God, remains the same. Hundreds and thousands and, yea, millions have died with their faith in this Book. There's something to it. It's a reality. It's true. It's genuine. It's the revelation of God. One of these days in Heaven, we can sit down and talk about all these things for a million years; then we'll have our chance to laugh at the evolutionists who have tried to make out of God nothing and make out of man something.

Let me read to you a tract that was published by Dr. Oswald J. Smith concerning the life and times and death of Charles Darwin. Dr. Oswald Smith says:

> It may surprise students of evolution who do not know, to learn that in the closing days of his life, Darwin returned to his faith in the Bible. Many a man as he approaches the end and consequently into the presence of God and eternity, has regretted both his views and conduct. Such a man was Darwin.
>
> The story is told by Lady Hope of Northfield, England, a wonderful Christian woman who was often at his bedside before he died. She herself writes it, and not only is it interesting—it is most enlightening. Here it is in her own words:
>
> "It was one of those glorious autumn afternoons that we sometimes enjoy in England, when I was asked to go and sit with the well-known professor, Charles Darwin. He was almost

bedridden sometime before he died. I used to feel, when I saw him, that his fine presence would have made a grand picture for our royal academy. But never did I think so more strongly than on this one particular occasion.

"He was sitting up in bed, wearing a soft, embroidered dressing gown of a rather rich purple shade. Propped up by pillows, he was gazing out on a far-stretching scene of woods and cornfields which glowed in the light of a marvelous sunset. His noble forehead and fine features seemed to be lit with pleasure as I entered the room.

"He waved his hand toward the window as he pointed out the scenes beyond while in the other hand he held an open Bible which he was always studying. 'What are you reading now?' I asked as I was seated by his bedside. 'Hebrews,' he answered. 'Still reading Hebrews, the royal book.' Then placing his finger on certain passages he commented on them.

"I made some illusions to the strong opinions expressed by many persons on this history of the creation, its grandeur and then their treatment of the earliest chapters of the book of Genesis. He seemed greatly distressed. His fingers twitched nervously, and a look of agony came over his face as he said, 'I was a young man with unformed ideas. I threw out queries, suggestions, wondering all the time over everything; and to my astonishment the ideas took like wildfire. People made a religion of them.'

"Then he paused; and after a few more sentences on the holiness of God and the grandeur of this book, looking at the Bible which he was holding tenderly all the time, he suddenly said, 'I have a summer house in the garden which holds about 30 people. It is over there (pointing to the open window). I want you very much to speak there. I know you read the Bible in the villages, but tomorrow afternoon I should like the servants on the place and a few of the neighbors to gather there. Would you speak to them?' 'What shall I speak about?' I asked. 'Jesus Christ,' he replied, 'and His salvation. Is not that the best theme? Then I want you to sing some hymns with them.'

"A wonderful look of brightness and animation on his face as he said this, I shall never forget. He added, 'If you take the meeting, at 3 o'clock this window will be open, and you will know that I am joining in with the singing.' "

According to this report published by the late Dr. Oswald

Smith of the People's Church in Canada, Charles Darwin returned to the faith. Do you remember the one statement, *". . .a young man with unformed ideas"*? Unformed, unfounded ideas that he just threw out, and the world took them up and made a religion of it. Now in his closing days, he's reading the Book and bragging on God, praising Christ, and saying, "If you take the meeting, at 3 o'clock this window will be open, and you will know that I am joining in with the singing."

Well, folks, stay by the old Book! Tonight there ought to be a renewal of our faith in the Book. Everything else is changing. Go yonder to your library tomorrow. You'll find all the texts on science that were written just a few years ago are now obsolete. But then pull out the old black Book, and you'll find something that's for today and yesterday and for tomorrow. And the things that are written in this Book never change because the Author never changes. God said, "I change not." "Jesus Christ the same yesterday, and to day, and for ever."

I'm staying on His side. I'm staying with Him, for I know He is going to see me through.

"And the Lord God formed man of the dust of the ground, and breathed into his nostrils the breath of life; and man became a living soul." O happy day that fixed my choice/On Thee, my Saviour and my God!"

I'm glad that our faith is anchored in the Book of books!

> **Within the ample volume lies**
> **The mystery of mysteries.**
> **Happiest they of human race**
> **To whom their God has given grace**
> **To read, to fear, to hope, to pray,**
> **To lift the latch, to force the way;**
> **But better had they ne'er been born**
> **That read to doubt or read to scorn.**
>
> —Sir Walter Scott

5

THE BIBLE

and Science

Paul writes to young Timothy, saying,

"O Timothy, keep that which is committed to thy trust, avoiding profane and vain babblings, and oppositions of science falsely so called: Which some professing have erred concerning the faith. Grace be with thee. Amen."—I Tim. 6:20,21.

The Bible and Science

In *This Week* magazine, the late Dr. Warner Von Braun wrote these words: "My life is predicated upon two basic principles: *faith* and *scientific reasoning.*" Notice the order: faith first. "Without faith, it is impossible to please God." I do not understand, nor do I believe anyone understands, the marvels of God's work. In the book of Hebrews, Paul writes concerning faith, "Through faith we understand that the worlds were framed by the word of God . . . ." The Bible does not tell us the *how* of creation; it tells us the *who* of creation.

We are now living in the most scientifically-oriented age in the history of mankind. There is abroad in the twentieth century an "information explosion." People are seeking information, desiring to learn as never before. More are enrolled in more schools than ever before in our history. I suppose there is more specialized study and specialized training in the twentieth century than in any part of our earlier history. It seems men all over the world are on a scientific hang-up. We might say that men are suffering a "technological fever." It appears that everything must pass the scientific test.

Not Science Worshipers

We will all admit that we are indebted to the men of science. In the field of medicine, we owe them a great debt. All of the modern miracle drugs have come into existence in the last twenty to twenty-five years.

We are indebted to the men of science in space travel, having gone to the moon and back.

We are indebted to the men of science in the field of communications. I can't understand how a man can speak on one side of the globe and his image be transmitted to the other side by satellite. I can't understand how a man's voice can be heard around the world. I can't understand how a brown cow can eat green grass and give white milk. A whole lot of things I don't understand.

Though we are indebted to the men of science, we must not equate scientific laws and scientific formula with the Bible. We must not equate scientists with God. We must not be guilty of worshiping at the shrine of science.

We must not offer sacrifices to the gods of knowledge. Incidentally, the word *science* stems from the root word which means "knowledge." We have a vast storehouse of knowledge in our world today. Yet man's knowledge of the universe is very limited.

While we speak of going into outer space to explore the reaches of space beyond us, in the depths of the ocean there are things that have never yet been uncovered or understood by man. From what I read and hear, I believe the next greatest exploration will be under the surface of the seas.

Science and Religion

We should understand from the start that science and religion are not in competition. Science and religion are more like companions. They only deal in two different areas of knowledge. Perhaps I can illustrate.

I have in my hand a nickel. Incased on a plate that we call a nickel is a picture of Monticello, the home of Thomas Jefferson. If I say to you, "A nickel has a picture of Monticello," I have told you only half the story. Turn over on the other side, and there is the picture of Thomas Jefferson himself.

Now, science looks at the nickel of knowledge and says, "Here is Monticello." But the Christian turns the coin over and sees the image of the great Designer who designed the design.

In our life, in our experience, we need both sides of the coin. Yes, we must have scientific data, scientific formula, scientific knowledge and scientific facts. But on the other hand, we must have a knowledge of God. Scientists tell us only what can be observed by natural senses, what man can see, feel or touch. But faith and spiritual perception go beyond that to the area of that which cannot be seen or felt or touched. Does not Paul speak in the book of Hebrews of seeing Him who is invisible? Does not Peter say, 'Whom having not seen, ye love, in whom, though now ye see him not, yet believing, ye rejoice with joy unspeakable and full of glory,' that one day we shall see Him? So bringing true science and Christianity together, we have both sides of the coin of knowledge.

Scientific Accuracy of the Bible

A modern theologian was quoted as saying, "Of course

there are scientific errors in the Bible. However, we can ex-
cuse such mistakes òn the grounds that the Bible is not a
textbook on science; therefore, we do not expect it to be scientifically accurate."

I agree with part of that statement—that is, that the Bible
is not a textbook on science. The Bible is basically the story
of God's love for sinful man. No wonder someone has penned,
"Wonderful things in the Bible I see:/This is the dearest, that
Jesus loves me." While the Bible is not a textbook on science,
I am convinced that, when it speaks scientifically, it speaks
accurately. The remainder of this modern theologian's statement to me is blasphemous. If the Bible is not scientifically
accurate, it is totally untrustworthy. If the Bible is not scientifically accurate, it is not accurate in any other area. And
if the Bible is not accurate, it is not inspired. And if the Bible
is not inspired, it is the mere imagination of man. And if it
is the mere imagination of man, it is untrue. And if the
Bible be not true, we are of all men most deceived and most
miserable.

The God who made and created and set in motion all of
the scientific marvels of the world system recorded them
precisely, systematically, correctly, accurately. The discov-
eries that man has made in the modern space age have not
surprised God. These principles, these formulas, have been
in operation since we read in Genesis, "In the beginning God
created the heaven and the earth." By imparting to him
knowledge and wisdom, God has permitted man to uncover,
to discover, a bit of knowledge here and a bit of knowledge
there.

What Does the Bible Say?

When we speak of the Bible and science, we must be certain of two things.

First, *we must be certain of what the Bible says.* A noted
preacher, who was also a scientist, one time put an adver-
tisement in papers all over the country offering a thousand

dollars to any person who could find one error in the Bible. You'd be amazed at the different reports that came from different places.

One lady, a graduate of the University of Michigan, wrote the preacher, "I demand my thousand dollars. I have found an error in the Bible. Most people believe, and most authorities agree, that the Garden of Eden," she went on to say, "is located in the Valley of Mesopotamia. And the Bible says [I'm still quoting her], that Adam and Eve were driven out of the Garden of Eden because they ate an apple. Give me my thousand dollars."

The noted preacher wrote back: "Dear Lady, read your Bible again. It does not say that Adam and Eve ate an apple and were driven out of the Garden of Eden. The Bible says they ate of the forbidden fruit of the tree of the knowledge of good and evil. It makes no mention of an apple."

She wrote back, "I couldn't find it anywhere, but I know it's in there. My teacher told me it was." We must be certain of our facts.

Second, *we must be certain of the scientific facts*. I'm not speaking of pseudo or false science, but true science, which is always progressive, always changing. If we, for some strange reason, felt it necessary to update the Bible scientifically, we would have to update it every year or two because science is forever progressing and changing.

I understand that in a library in Paris, France, there are three and one-half miles of books on science, and every single one of them is now obsolete. A science book that was written ten years ago is already nine years obsolete.

Not so with the Bible. The last book of the Bible is the book of the Revelation, written almost nineteen hundred years ago, and it has never changed. The Bible has never been and shall never be obsolete. It shall always be *absolute*. Jesus said, "Heaven and earth shall pass away, but my words shall not pass away." The Word is forever settled in Heaven. The Word of the Lord endureth forever.

No Contradictions

In the year 1861, the French Academy of Science published a list of fifty-one scientific facts that had reportedly contradicted the Bible. Today there is not a scientist in the world who believes any one of those fifty-one so-called scientific facts. In all the years that the Bible was being written—over sixteen hundred years—forty different writers all agreed. That's the most remarkable thing, the most fantastic thing that we ever heard of. A most amazing thing! Not one single writer contradicted another. Not one single writer included the weird ideas of his day. The Bible is inspired.

The Bible and Science

Let us look briefly at some of the notable examples of the scientific accuracy of the Bible and the absurd inaccuracy of science. In Acts 7:22 I read, "And Moses was learned in all the wisdom of the Egyptians, and was mighty in words and in deeds." The archaeologists have uncovered the libraries, the universities, the schools, the textbooks that Moses studied in Egypt in the fourteenth century before Christ. We know from the findings of archaeology exactly what Moses was taught. He was well versed, according to this verse. He was well versed in the scientific facts of his day. Moses learned Egyptian cosmogony, that is, the science of creation. In Moses' day, the Egyptians believed that the earth hatched out of an egg. Here's an egg that has wings flying around in a cosmic atmosphere. Through the process of mitosis, that is, the division of the cells, the egg cracks open, and out falls the earth. Fantastic! Absurd! Weird!

When I go to the book that Moses wrote telling me about the creation of the earth, I read no such thing as a flying egg hatching out. I read nothing about a hatchery. What do I find? These words: "In the beginning God created the heaven and the earth." But Moses, no doubt, was taught when he went to school that the earth hatched out of an egg.

The Bible is inspired, and Moses got his information from God, not from the classroom.

Moses not only had a class in cosmogony, but he had a class in astronomy. The professor of astronomy of Moses' day believed that the sun got its light from the earth. Here is the earth, yonder is the sun. And all the light that the sun has comes from the earth, according to the astronomer of Moses' day.

But when I look in the book that Moses wrote about the lesser and the greater light, I don't find anything like that. I find Moses saying that God made two lights, the sun and the moon, one to rule by day and the other to rule by night.

In the Apollo series in space, millions and millions and millions of dollars were spent to send men to the moon to find out where it came from. I could have given them a 98-cent Bible. And in Genesis 1, they could have read verses 16 and 17 and learned that God created the moon. Then all those millions could have been spent on something else.

Isn't it wonderful how accurate the Bible is scientifically? When God created the heaven and the earth, He placed the moon about 240,000 miles away from the earth. You know that the moon governs the tides. Had the moon been placed only fifty thousand miles from the earth, tidal waves would go over the top of the Rocky Mountains. Can you imagine walking out one day and seeing from the West and from the East the Atlantic and the Pacific Oceans converging at the Rocky Mountains, two walls of water perhaps fourteen thousand feet high! In three days the Rocky Mountains would be washed away, if the moon were only fifty thousand miles away. God knew what He was doing when He placed it where He did.

When the bell rang and Moses left the class of astronomy, he went over to anthropology. There he had a professor who taught a weird idea. Where did man come from? I can imagine Moses might have been listening when some little fellow put his hand up and said, "Teacher, tell us about

where man came from." And the old professor of anthropology in Egypt said, "Well, son, there was along the banks of
the Nile a little white worm, and man sprang from a little
white worm." Well, that's what they taught Moses when he
went to school in Egypt.

But when Moses sat down to write the inspired account
of creation, I don't read anything about the Nile River and
little white worms crawling around. I read in Genesis 2:7,
"And the Lord God formed man of the dust of the ground,
and breathed into his nostrils the breath of life; and man
became a living soul."

In the year 1615, William Harvey discovered the circulatory
system of the blood—an amazing find. William Harvey said,
"All the processes of life are in the bloodstream." But
thousands of years before that, Moses had said, in Leviticus
17:11, "For the life of the flesh is in the blood." So science
finally caught up with Moses and said, "Look! Here is the
circulatory system. All of the life processes are in the blood."
Moses knew that and said so hundreds of years before, in
Leviticus 17!

Babylonian Science and Isaiah

As we leave the science of Egypt, we journey to the science
of Babylon. The man Isaiah, who lived in the eighth century
before Christ, wrote against the background of Babylonian
science. According to Babylonian anthropology, life and the
earth came into existence in this way. A teacher in Isaiah's
day might have said: There was a war, a struggle between
Marduk, the Babylonian god, and a monster named Tiamat.
And the Babylonian god Marduk overpowered Tiamat and
cast him out of the atmosphere, and his corpse became the
earth. Marduk spit, and man was formed. Man spit, and
woman was formed. The woman spit, and the animals were
formed. Amazing, isn't it!

Isaiah could have learned that when he went to school,
because the influence of Babylon had reached over into

Jerusalem where Isaiah was yet a young man. Yet when I turn to the book of Isaiah I find no such weird, fantastic idea, but I read in chapter 45, verse 12, where God says, "I have made the earth, and created man upon it."

Isaiah was born in the year 760 B.C. In his day no man believed the earth was round, yet he wrote in chapter 40 and verse 22:

"It is he that sitteth upon the circle of the earth, and the inhabitants thereof are as grasshoppers; that stretcheth out the heavens as a curtain, and spreadeth them out as a tent to dwell in."

It is now a scientific fact that the earth is round. However, Isaiah knew it long before the scientists, because God revealed it to him through the process of inspiration.

Job and Science

In the book of Job, reported to be the oldest book in the Bible, we read in 26:7, "He stretcheth out the north over the empty place, and hangeth the earth upon nothing." In Job's day men thought that the earth rested on a solid foundation. The Egyptians said it rested on five great pillars. The Greeks held that the earth rested on the shoulders of Atlas, a great giant. The Hindus said it rested on an elephant, which rested on a turtle, which was swimming in a cosmic ocean. Such was the latest scientific data in Job's day. Yet Job said, 'God hangeth the earth upon nothing.'

A Look Into the New Testament

Paul wrote in I Corinthians 15:39, "All flesh is not the same flesh: but there is one kind of flesh of men, another flesh of beasts, another of fishes, and another of birds." The word for flesh is *protoplasm,* and the scientists vowed Paul was wrong, declaring all protoplasm was the same. Paul said there were various kinds—one protoplasm in men, a different protoplasm in beasts, another kind in fish, and even another kind in birds.

Later, science discovered that Paul was correct. There is a difference in the flesh (protoplasm) of man and that of animals. This is proof positive that the Bible is scientifically accurate.

The Earth Is Winding Down

An amazing truth appears in the book of Hebrews concerning the "winding down of the earth."

"And, Thou, Lord, in the beginning hast laid the foundation of the earth; and the heavens are the works of thine hands: They shall perish; but thou remainest; and they all shall wax old as doth a garment; And as a vesture shalt thou fold them up, and they shall be changed: but thou art the same, and thy years shall not fail."—Heb. 1:10-12.

In his book, *Wider Aspects of Cosmogony*, Sir James Jean said, "The universe is like a clock winding down." It is true that every time energy is dispelled, the universe "breaks down," and it will continue to do so until it finally disintegrates, as the Bible says it will. The scientists have changed their thinking about the earth. At one time they thought it would last billions of years. At present, they do not think so. Again they are catching up with the Bible.

Paul declared the dissolution of the earth long before science arrived at the truth. And the psalmist said it long before the apostle did:

"Of old hast thou laid the foundation of the earth: and the heavens are the work of thy hands. They shall perish, but thou shalt endure: yea, all of them shall wax old like a garment; as a vesture shalt thou change them, and they shall be changed."—Ps. 102:25,26.

Let us, then, conclude that, even though the Bible is not a textbook on science, when it speaks scientifically, it speaks accurately. "It's in the Book." May God bless all who believe His inspired Word!

6

THE BIBLE

and the Deity of Christ

"**A**nd without controversy great is the mystery of godliness: God was manifest in the flesh, justified in the Spirit, seen of angels, preached unto the Gentiles, believed on in the world, received up into glory."—I Tim. 3:16.

This is the life of Christ in a nutshell.

Attacks Upon Deity

Any attack upon the Bible, the Word of God, is an attack upon the deity of the Lord Jesus Christ. In John, chapter 14 and verse 9, Jesus said, "He that hath seen me hath seen the Father." Jesus said, "I and my Father are one."

When the liberals attack the inspiration of the Scriptures, they attack the deity of Jesus Christ.

When the atheists attack the existence of God, they attack the deity of Jesus Christ.

When the evolutionists attack the Genesis account of creation, they attack the deity of Jesus Christ.

When the skeptics attack the miracles in the Bible, they attack the deity of the Lord Jesus Christ.

When the infidels attack the virgin birth of Jesus, they attack the deity of the Lord.

Nothing New

The war of attempted annihilation against Jesus Christ is not new. It began in the long ago. Satan himself launched the first campaign in the Garden of Eden when he lied to our first parents, Adam and Eve.

Pharaoh launched a campaign in Egypt when he attempted to destroy all the male children of Israel.

Nebuchadnezzar launched a campaign in Jerusalem when he attempted to wipe out Judah, the tribe that was prophesied to bring into the world in the flesh the Lord Jesus Christ.

Herod the Great launched an attack in his campaign in Bethlehem when he issued a decree for the slaughter of all the infants.

In the twentieth century the battle rages on.

It is fought by professors in the classroom.

It is fought by preachers in the pulpit.

It is fought by profaners in the street.

Permit me to read to you from a book entitled *In Defense of the Faith* by the famed pastor of the First Baptist Church of Dallas, Texas. Dr. Criswell writes concerning some of the liberals and infidels in so-called Christian schools and seminaries. I quote Dr. Criswell who quotes another source, *The Leaven of the Sadducees*, by Ernest Gordon.

> One of our noble Christian seminaries had a professor who said, "An intelligent man who now affirms his faith in miracles can hardly know what intellectual honesty means. The hypothesis of God has become superfluous in religion. Jesus

did not transcend the limits of purely human."

Another great Christian theological school had a professor who said, "We shall hardly bandy words about the finality of Christ. The field is open for anyone at any time to mean more to men than Jesus has meant. He was a mere human being. He was the child of his people and of his time."

A far-famed Christian college had a professor who wrote, "Whether Jesus ever lived is a historical question that is interesting, but it is not fundamental to religion, and if it be suggested in criticism that you then have a Christian religion without a historic Jesus, may I suggest that if Jesus was all that he so generously claimed, or that is so generously claimed of him, he ought not to be so sensitive about his own name or himself."

A great seminary had a professor who said, "I believe that the whole view of the Bible with its theory of a chosen people, special revelation, and prophecies is utterly unconvincing and basically vicious."

Possibly the most famous seminary in America had a professor who said, "I do not believe that the religion of tomorrow will have any more place for prayer than it will have for any other form of magic."

Another who said, "As far as I am concerned, the idea of God plays no part in my religion."

Another who added, "Where the old religion made the supreme object God, the new religion makes it humanity. Sociology takes the place of theology, and an improved social order replaces the belief in immortality."

The editor of the *Chicago Daily News* wrote in an editorial:

We are stuck with the hypocrisy and the treachery and the attacks on Christianity. This is a free country and a free age, and men can say what they choose about religion, but this is not what we arraigned these divinity professors for. Is there no place to assail Christianity but a divinity school? Is there no one to write infidel books but professors of Christian theology? Is a theological seminary an appropriate place for a general massacre of Christian doctrines? We are not championing either Christianity or infidelity, but only condemning infidels masquerading as men of God and Christian teachers.

Denying the Faith

I heard an outstanding man of God and pastor of long standing say not long ago that he could count on one hand the seminaries in the United States that are still true to the inspired Word of God.

We're living in an hour when the professors are fighting in the classroom against the deity of the Lord Jesus. As I stated earlier, any attack against the Bible, any attack against the creation, any attack against inspiration, and any attack against miracles is an attack directly against the Lord Jesus Christ. Preachers in the pulpits are doing the same.

The name Bob Ingersoll will register with some of you. Bob Ingersoll was one of the most infamous infidels this country has ever known. He made it his business to go up and down the length and breadth of this nation denouncing the Bible, denouncing inspiration, denouncing the virgin birth, and denouncing the deity of the Lord Jesus Christ.

One day someone asked him after he had quit doing that, "Why, Mr. Ingersoll, have you quit going across the country denouncing the Bible and denouncing the Faith and denouncing Christ?" And his answer was, "The divinity professors in the classrooms and the preachers in the pulpits are doing a fine job without my help. I need no longer denounce the Faith."

The danger of denouncing the Faith is the fact that it is coming from so-called scholasticism—the so-called intellectuals of our day.

If some bum who just jumped off a railroad car would come up to you and say, "I don't believe God exists," that wouldn't disturb you.

If some long-haired hippie trying to find his way would come to you and say, "Christ was not the Son of God," that wouldn't disturb you.

But when a man of the cloth, when a man in high divinical circles stands in the pulpit or in a classroom and denies the inspiration of the Bible, denies the virgin birth of Christ and denies the deity of the Lord, that should cause you concern. And that's what is happening all over the world. It is difficult to choose a college in our day where you can trust the theology department or the department of religion.

God help us to come back to the hour when we make our stand for the blessed old Book, the Book that men have lived by and died by. This is our creed. This is our only and final rule of authority, and this is the blessed Book of God, and it tells us about the blessed Christ of God.

Is Christ God?

The crux of the whole matter is this: Jesus Christ is either God or He is not God. He is either right or wrong. He is either good or evil. He is either true of false.

Is Christ an impostor?

Is Christ an impersonator?

Is Christ a usurper?

Is Christ an imitator?

Is Christ a blasphemer?

Is Christ a fraud?

Is Christ a paranoid?

Is Christ a pretender?

If He is not the Son of God, He is all this and much more. If Jesus Christ is not the Son of God. . .He has deceived countless millions; He has blasphemed the Almighty; He has desecrated all that is sacred; He has made a laughingstock of multiplied countless millions of believers; He has falsely represented God; He has nullified the doctrine of the Trinity; He has scandalized the truth of God; He has invalidated the writings of the prophets.

To deny the deity of the Lord Jesus is to deny the ability of God, the truth of God, the creation of God, the worship of God, the power of God, the Word of God, the salvation of God, the mercy of God, the wisdom of God, the grace of God and the love of God.

To strip Christ of His deity would be to put the demons back into the demoniac. It would mean to put the fever back into the sick. It would mean to put blindness back into the beggar. It would mean to put Lazarus back at the rich man's gate. It would mean to put the dead back into their graves, never to live again.

To take the deity away from Christ would be to take the wine out of the waterpots in Cana of Galilee. It would be to take the fish and loaves out of the boy's basket. It would be to take the fish out of the fisherman's net, the brightness out of the sun, the reflection out of the moon, the fragrance out of the flowers and the light out of all the stars.

To erase the deity of Christ would be to erase all rhythm from all poetry. It would erase the music from all songs. It would erase the beauty from all art. It would erase the name of every born-again, blood-washed, redeemed soul whose name is recorded in the Lamb's Book of Life.

To destroy His deity means you will have to destroy the Bible. You will have to destroy the church. You will have to destroy the home. You will have to destroy government. You will have to destroy civilization. You would have to destroy history. You would have to destroy prophecy.

To eradicate His deity, you would have to uproot all the trees, extinguish all the fires, dry up all the rivers, evaporate all oceans, eliminate all the elements, dissolve all matter, eradicate all energy, destroy all life, disintegrate the earth, darken the sun, denounce the truth, deny the miracles, desecrate the Faith, and ultimately dethrone God.

If you were to rob Jesus Christ of His deity, you would have to break up all the homes He has salvaged. You would have to disease all the bodies He has healed. You would have to kill all the dead He has raised from the grave. You would have to disease and twist the limbs of all those whom He hath straightened out. You would have to inebriate all the drunkards He has sobered. You would have to emaciate all the weaklings He has strengthened. You would have to shatter all the dreams He has fulfilled. You would have to break all the hearts He has mended. You would have to tear-stain all the eyes He has dried. You would have to unsave all the souls He has saved.

If you dissolve His deity, you would have to divorce all the couples who have married in His name. You would have to destroy all the documents that have been dated from His birth. You would have to denounce all the doctrines taught in His Book. You would have to defrock all the preachers who have been ordained to His Gospel. You would have to de-church all the people who have been added to His blessed body.

Ladies and gentlemen, none of this is necessary. None of this is possible. None of this can be done, nor should it ever be attempted because Jesus Christ is the Son of the Living God. Peter said, "Thou art the Christ, the Son of the living God." And Jesus said to him, "Blessed art thou, Simon Bar-jona: for flesh and blood hath not revealed it unto thee, but my Father which is in heaven."

What I am giving you does not come out of the books of science. It does not come out of the books of knowledge. It does not come out of the books of learning. It comes out of the Book of God. Jesus Christ is God in the flesh. What a Saviour is our Saviour!

You need not blush to speak His name. You need not stutter or stammer to praise His wonderful Word. His story is written on every page of human history. His image is stamped on every member of Adam's race. His power is manifest in every motion of the universe. Jesus Christ is God! It is declared in John, chapter 1, verses 1, 2 and 14:

"In the beginning was the Word, and the Word was with God, and the Word was God. The same was in the beginning with God. . . . And the Word was made flesh, and dwelt among us, (and we beheld his glory, the glory as of the only begotten of the Father,) full of grace and truth."

It is written in Colossians 2:9, "For in him dwelleth all the fulness of the Godhead bodily"—God the Father, God the Son, and God the blessed Spirit. In the name of the thrice holy God, I declare to you that Jesus Christ is God.

Jesus Is God

He always has been God.

He always shall be God.

God never changes.

God never diminishes.

He will always be the same.

Jesus Christ was God in the world above.

He was God on the plains of Mamre as He spoke to Abraham.

He was God on Mount Sinai when He gave the commandments and the law to Moses.

He was God in the womb of the Virgin Mary.

He was God in the manger at Bethlehem.

He was God in the carpenter's shop at Nazareth.

He was God in the boat at Lake Galilee.

He was God in the Temple at Jerusalem.

He was God on the Mount of Transfiguration.

He was God in the Garden of Gethsemane as He prayed, "Let this cup pass from me: nevertheless, not my will, but as thou wilt."

He was God on the cross as He cried out, "It is finished."

He was God in the tomb of Joseph as He lay still in death.

He was God on the morning of the resurrection as He broke asunder the bands of death and came out triumphantly over death, the grave and Hell.

He was God on the Mount of Olives as His feet left that sacred spot.

He was God in the cloud of ascension as He went away.

He is God at the right hand of the throne now.

He will be God coming again as He comes in flaming fire to take vengeance upon all who know not Him and who have never trusted Him as Saviour.

Unmistakably Divine

History declares His deity. Prophecy accents His deity. Christianity testifies of His deity. Philosophy reasons of His deity. Literature writes about His deity. And music sings of His deity.

To explain Him is impossible. To ignore Him is disastrous. To reject Him is fatal. But to know Him is to love Him, and to love Him is to believe Him, and to believe Him is to be saved. Human speech is too limited to describe Him. The human mind is too finite to comprehend Him. The human heart is too small to contain Him.

He was God in the flesh during His days upon earth. When He worked, God labored with human hands. When He walked, God traveled on human feet. Jesus Christ is God! The deity of the Lord Jesus Christ is the one doctrine upon which all the other doctrines of the Bible either stand or fall.

I repeat, if He be not the Son of God, He is the greatest impostor and blasphemer the world has ever known. He surely was a man suffering under great delusions if He were not God.

Who else but God could say, "Thy sins be forgiven thee"? Who else but God could say, "Go thy way and sin no more"? Who else but God could say, "I am the way, the truth, and the life"? Who else but God could say, "I am Alpha and Omega"? About whom else could it be said, "Neither is there salvation in any other: for there is none other name under heaven given among men, whereby we must be saved"? Who else could claim to be the Light of the world but God? Who else could be the bread of life but God? Who else could be the water of life but God?

Who else could say, "I am the resurrection, and the life: he that believeth in me, though he were dead, yet shall he live: And whosoever liveth and believeth in me shall never die"? Who else could say, "Come unto me, all ye that labour and are heavy laden, and I will give you rest"? Who else could say, "Take my yoke upon you, and learn of me; for I am meek and lowly in heart: and ye shall find rest unto your souls"? Who else could say, "Behold, I come quickly; and my reward is with me"? None but God! None but God in the flesh, and Jesus Christ was just as much God as though He had never been man, and just as much man as though He had never been God.

Deity Confirmed

The deity of Christ is confirmed in seven basic ways. First, **His deity is confirmed by the *names* given Him.** He is called "God" in Hebrews 1:8. He is called the "Son of God" in Matthew 16:16. He is called the "Lord" in Acts 16:31.

Second, **His deity is confirmed by the *worship* that is ascribed to Him.** Men and angels worship Him. Let me read it to you from the Revelation, chapter 5, beginning at verse 11:

"And I beheld, and I heard the voice of many angels round about the throne and the beasts and the elders: and the number of them was ten thousand times ten thousand, and thousands of thousands; Saying with a loud voice, Worthy is the Lamb that was slain to receive power, and riches, and wisdom, and strength, and honour, and glory, and blessing."

And I read in Philippians, chapter 2:

"Let this mind be in you, which was also in Christ Jesus: Who, being in the form of God, thought it not robbery to be equal with God: But made himself of no reputation, and took upon him the form of a servant, and was made in the likeness of men: And being found in fashion as a man, he humbled himself, and became obedient unto death, even the death of the cross. Wherefore God also hath highly exalted him, and given him a name which is above every name: That at the name of Jesus every knee should bow, of things in heaven, and things in earth, and things under the earth; And that every tongue should confess that Jesus

Christ is Lord, to the glory of God the Father."

Men everywhere one day shall worship Him when the angels fall down before Him ascribing to Him all majesty and glory and might and power and wisdom from every tribe on this terrestrial globe. Out of every kindred on the earth shall men come to pay honor to Him. Bless His wonderful name! Love Him? Yes! Adore Him? Yes! Worship Him? Yes! Crown Him Lord of all? Yes! Bring forth the royal diadem, and crown Him Lord of all!

The third fact that confirms His deity is His *equality* with the Father. In John, chapter 5, He is seen as being equal with the Father in working, in wisdom, in His power to resurrect the dead, in His authority to judge, in His position of honor, and in His ability to give life. He is equal with the Father.

The fourth great fact that confirms His deity is His *virgin birth*. In Genesis 3:15 it is prophesied that the Seed of the woman would bruise the head of Satan, the serpent. The old rabbi used to wonder about that verse. The Seed of the woman? Unheard of! The seed comes from the man. But then 750 years before Christ was born, Isaiah took the prophetic pen in hand and wrote, "The Lord himself shall give you a sign; Behold, a virgin shall conceive, and bear a son, and shall call his name Immanuel," which means "God with us." In Luke 1:35 when the angel made the announcement to Mary, he said,

"The Holy Ghost shall come upon thee, and the power of the Highest shall overshadow thee: therefore also that holy thing which shall be born of thee shall be called the Son of God."

The virgin birth is the most important doctrine that supports the deity of the Lord Jesus Christ upon which all other doctrines fall or stand.

If Jesus Christ be not born of a virgin, there is no Trinity;

for He is the second person of the Trinity. If Jesus Christ be not born of a virgin, there is no resurrection; for He is the resurrection. If Jesus Christ be not born of a virgin, Christianity is only a myth that will in the end succumb to its own deception and be buried beneath the ashes of its own presumption.

Jesus Christ was virgin-born. It matters not what all the infidels and agnostics and unbelievers and college professors and "baboon chasers" and D. D.'s and PH. D.'s and everybody else say, I believe He was born of a virgin because the Bible says so. I believe He was born of a virgin because He lives in my heart. I believe! I believe! I believe that Christ is the virgin-born, sinless, perfect Son of the living God.

The fifth fact that confirms His deity is His *sacrificial death* upon the cross. I read in I Corinthians, chapter 15 and verse 3: "Christ died for our sins." If He were not the divine Son of God, His death would be meaningless. His death would mean no more than your death. He must be, and He *is*, the Son of God because He died a sacrificial death upon the cross. Peter said in his first epistle, chapter 2, "Who his own self bare our sins in his own body on the tree, that we, being dead to sins, should live unto righteousness: by whose stripes ye were healed."

The sixth outstanding fact that confirms His deity is His glorious *resurrection* from among the dead. I read in Romans 1:4 that He is declared to be the Son of God by the resurrection from the dead. Before Christ there was no resurrection. Until Christ comes again, there shall not be any resurrection; for He *is* the resurrection and the life.

The seventh fact that confirms His deity is His triumphant *return*. Sweeter words were never spoken than these from John's Gospel, chapter 14:

"Let not your heart be troubled: ye believe in God, believe also in me. In my Father's house are many mansions: if it were not so, I would have told you. I go to prepare a place for you. And if I go and prepare a place for you, I will come

again, and receive you unto myself; that where I am, there ye may be also."

The deity of the Lord Jesus Christ is the central thought and the central fiber and the central doctrine of the Bible.

Footnote

I have a footnote and I am through: The deity of Christ is confirmed by the *testimony of men who died clinging to the belief that Jesus Christ is the Saviour.*

Mr. Pat Zondervan of the Zondervan Publishing House in Michigan often goes across the country making an appeal for the Gideons International, placing Bibles all over the world. In one of his recent presentations of the ministry of the Gideons, he held up a little Testament that had been taken off the body of a dead soldier in Vietnam—a marine from the state of Georgia. When he held it up, everybody noticed that there was a hole all the way through the little Testament. There was blood on every page—the blood of a soldier fallen in battle. And when he turned to the last page, there was written in the trembling handwriting of a dying soldier these words: *"I, Wilton Thomas, take Jesus Christ as my personal Saviour."* He signed his name, Wilton Thomas, and died clinging to the belief that Jesus Christ is the divine Son of God.

I believe it! It's in the Book!

7

THE BIBLE

and the Magnificence of Christ

"**T**he queen of the south shall rise up in the judgment with this generation, and shall condemn it: for she came from the uttermost parts of the earth to hear the wisdom of Solomon; and, behold, a greater than Solomon is here."—Matt. 12:42.

Christ, Greater Than Solomon

"Behold, a greater than Solomon is here." You may ask, "Why did Jesus compare Himself to Solomon?" I answer, Of all the men in history, King Solomon of Israel was one of the greatest. His greatness was seen in a number of ways. I mention just five.

One: his greatness was seen in his *riches*. Solomon was one of the richest men who ever lived. His income per year in gold amounted to twenty billion dollars, and this is besides his mining, his manufacturing and his investments.

Second, his greatness was seen by his *army,* his *navy,* his *chariots* and his *horses.* Solomon, who lived almost one thousand years before Christ, had fourteen hundred chariots, twelve hundred horsemen and four thousand stables in which to keep his horses.

Third, his greatness was seen in his *wisdom.* He was wiser than the men of Egypt, Babylon, Assyria and Persia.

Fourth, his greatness was seen in his *accomplishments.* He built the Temple. Estimates of the value of the Temple in our currency have gone anywhere from three and one-half to five billion dollars. He built houses. He built cities. He built stables. He built aqueducts. He built pools. He built tunnels. Solomon accomplished many wonderful and mighty things.

Lastly, one of the most notable ways Solomon's greatness was seen was in his *versatility.* There never lived a more versatile man. In addition to being the king of Israel, he was an author, an architect, an arbitrator and an administrator. He was a builder, a biologist, a botanist and a banker. He was a poet, a philosopher, a philanthropist and a preacher. He was a soldier, a scientist and a singer.

One day the queen of the South, the Queen of Sheba, went to see King Solomon. The Bible says he answered every question she asked him. And when she had seen his wealth and might and majesty and glory, she said something like this to King Solomon:

> In my country there was a story told—a story of your greatness, power and might, a story of your army and chariots, a story of your silver and gold, a story of the great house of the Lord you built and a story of the great houses and cities you engineered and administrated. I believed that story, but now that I have seen it all, the half has not yet been told.

If we could see Christ by the eye of faith, if we could see His majestic glory, how it sits enthroned upon the Saviour's brow; if we could but see the marvels of Heaven and the marvels of the glory of Christ, I am sure we would turn to the world and say, "Though I read it in the Book and heard it from the lips of the preacher, the half has never been told, for a greater than Solomon is here."

The Greatness of Christ

First, He is greater than Solomon in His *position.* Solomon was an earthly king. Jesus Christ is a heavenly King.

He was greater in His *possessions.* Solomon made twenty billion dollars a year in gold, besides his mining, manufacturing and investments. But Jesus Christ is not only the Owner of the cattle on a thousand hills but the Possessor of Heaven and earth, and all the riches of all the mines and all the wealth of the world is in His hands. We are serving the Christ of God who is far richer than Solomon could ever be.

He is greater than Solomon in His *power.* Solomon's army defeated Egypt, Tyre and Sidon. In His majestic glory, Jesus Christ, when He returns in revelation with His saints to reign upon the earth, shall destroy all the nations of earth singlehandedly at the battle of Armageddon. The Bible tells us there shall go forth out of His mouth a sharp sword, and with that sword He shall smite the nations of the earth.

This is our Christ. This is our Solomon. This is our King, great in power.

He is greater than Solomon in His *performance.* Solomon gave to the King of Tyre twenty cities. He gave to the Queen of Sheba more things than could be counted or named or numbered. But beloved, Jesus Christ will give the title deed to this earth to us in the day John speaks of in Revelation 5.

The seven-sealed book was in the hand of Him who sat upon the throne, and John began to weep because no one was found worthy to open that book and to break those seals. Then there stepped up before the throne of Almighty God the Lamb for sinners slain, the Lion of the tribe of Judah. He took that book and opened every seal. And in the opening of the seals, He gives back to us everything Satan took away from us in the Garden of Eden. A title deed to the world is ours through the magnificent performance of Jesus Christ.

Jesus Christ is greater in His *preaching.* Solomon was a great preacher. He preached the message of dedication when the Temple was completed, a message which contained words of wisdom that stirred the hearts of a great nation like Israel. But our Lord Jesus Christ stood on the mount and delivered His famous sermon that we call "The Sermon on the Mount." In that sermon He laid down the laws of the greatest kingdom that shall ever be—the kingdom of Christ upon the earth.

Jesus Christ is greater than Solomon in His *philosophy.* Solomon's philosophy can be found in one verse in the book of Ecclesiastes: "Vanity of vanities, saith the Preacher. . .all is vanity." The philosophy of Jesus Christ can be summarized in two verses:

"Lay not up for yourselves treasures upon earth, where moth and rust doth corrupt, and where thieves break through and steal: But lay up for yourselves treasures in heaven, where neither moth nor rust doth corrupt, and where thieves do not break through nor steal."—Matt. 6:19,20.

Solomon spoke of one economy, and Christ spoke of another. The wisest investment you can make is an investment in the lives of people who have surrendered themselves to Jesus Christ to take the Gospel to the ends of the earth. One day when all that is on earth is tarnished and when all that is in this world has decayed, deteriorated, rusted and been worn out, the things we do not see and the things we grasp by faith are the things that will last for eternity.

What a glorious treasure is ours in Christ Jesus! And there will be no rust and moth and thieves to break through and deteriorate our treasure in Heaven.

Jesus Christ is greater than Solomon in His *program.* Solomon's program embraced only time and concerned only the nation Israel. The program of Jesus Christ embraces eternity. I read in the Bible, "From everlasting to everlasting, thou art God." Long before the morning stars sang together, long before Gabriel sounded his trumpet in the Glory world, our Lord Jesus Christ was from the beginning the *very* God man. "In the beginning was the Word, and the Word was with God, and the Word was God." From everlasting to everlasting, world without end, is Christ, embracing not only time, but eternity, embracing not only one nation, but people from every tribe, every kindred and every continent on the earth. This is the program of Christ. "Whosoever will, let him come and drink of the water of life freely." This is the program of Christ—worldwide and universal—not only for time, but for eternity.

Jesus Christ is greater than Solomon in His *policy.* The policy of Solomon was to draft men to serve him and the nation Israel. The policy of Christ is to call volunteers to serve Him around the world.

Jesus Christ was greater than Solomon in His *promises.* Solomon promised his followers social security. Jesus Christ promises His followers eternal security.

"My sheep hear my voice, and I know them, and they follow me: And I give unto them eternal life; and they shall never perish, neither shall any man pluck them out of my hand. My Father, which gave them me, is greater than all; and no man is able to pluck them out of my Father's hand."—John 10:27-29.

What a policy! What a promise—eternity with Christ!

Jesus Christ is greater than Solomon in His *proclamation.* The proclamation of Solomon can be summarized in one verse from the book of Ecclesiastes—2:9, "I was great, and increased more than all that were before me in Jerusalem." The proclamation of Jesus Christ can be summarized in His divine claims. Jesus said, "I am the way, the truth, and the life." Jesus said, "I am the door of the sheep." "I am the Good Shepherd." "I am the bread of life." "I am the resurrection and the life." "I am Alpha and Omega, the beginning and the end, the first and the last." And in the Revelation He says, to summarize it all, "I am he that liveth, and was dead; and behold, I am alive for evermore, amen; and have the keys of hell and of death."

What a proclamation! Who else could say to a poor lost sinner, "Go thy way and sin no more"? Who else could say to a fallen woman, "Neither do I condemn thee: go, and sin no more"? This is the proclamation of Christ, "Whosoever shall call upon the name of the Lord shall be saved."

Jesus Christ is greater than Solomon in His *prayer*. Solomon prayed in the dedication of the Temple, "Oh, Lord, forgive the people who have sinned against thee." From the cross, with parching lips, with wounds that drained His blood, with a body that was totally battered and bruised, Jesus Christ prayed, "Father, forgive them, for they know not what they do." This prayer of our Saviour is a prayer for forgiveness. And my friend, if you are ever forgiven of your sins, it will be because Jesus prayed for you. If you are ever saved, it will be because Jesus prayed for you. If you ever go to Heaven, it will be because Jesus prayed for you. He is greater than Solomon in His prayer.

He is greater than Solomon in His *provision*. Solomon promised and provided for his followers food, clothing and shelter. Jesus Christ provides rest for the weary, strength for the weak, hope for the hopeless, health for the sick, mercy for the living, grace for the dying and an expense-paid trip to Heaven to everyone who will believe. What a provision!

He is greater than Solomon in His *payment*. Solomon paid in billions of dollars for his Temple. Jesus Christ paid in His own precious blood for His temple.

Jesus Christ is greater than Solomon in His *peace*. Solomon brought peace to Israel. Jesus Christ, our Solomon, shall bring peace to the ends of the earth.

Jesus Christ is greater than Solomon in His *prominence.* Solomon's prominence is seen in the fact that the kings of the East came to learn of his wisdom. The prominence of Jesus Christ is seen in the fact that one day the kingdoms of this world shall become the kingdoms of our Lord, and He shall rule them with a rod of iron.

> **Jesus shall reign where'er the sun**
> **Does his successive journeys run;**
> **His kingdom spread from shore to shore,**
> **Till moons shall wax and wane no more.**
> **Behold the islands with their kings,**
> **And Europe her finest tribute brings.**
> **From north to south the princes meet**
> **To pay their homage at His feet.**

Jesus Christ is greater than Solomon in His *person.* Solomon was the wise, witty and wealthy son of David. Jesus Christ is the pure, perfect and powerful Son of God. Behold, a greater than Solomon is here! He is here to strengthen you if you are weak. He is here to give rest if you are weary. He is here to lift you if you are fallen. He is here to cheer you if you are sad. He is here to save you if you are lost.

"Behold, a greater than Solomon is here."

8

THE BIBLE

and the Unchanging Christ

"Jesus Christ the same yesterday, and to day, and for ever."—Heb. 13:8.

A Changing World

The most permanent thing in all our world is change. We're living in the midst of a changing world. Would it not be interesting to go back and trace the history of Western civilization? How much civilization has changed! Even in our own nation, in the two hundred years of being a nation, so much has changed. Has it occurred to you how much change fads and fashions undergo? It's hard to keep up with the styles that change week after week and month after month and day after day.

Sadly enough, many churches have changed and geared their program to a streamlined and worldly one in order to attract people. This is a dangerous trend. When the church wants to become like the world or resorts to that which tickles the ear, excites the flesh and motivates nonessentials, we've reached a very dangerous hour in the history of the church.

One thing I appreciated about Dr. B. R. Lakin was, at his death, he was preaching the same way he was preaching fifty years ago. And believe me, evangelism has changed in the last fifty years.

But some evangelists have not changed with the time. Thank God, some churches have not changed with the time. I feel we ought to have a national and international calling back to the New Testament way of getting things done. We can't improve on the Acts way of building churches. God did not write a book that was applicable only for the first century. God did not write us a Bible that was true only a hundred or five hundred or a thousand or two thousand years ago. God gave us a Book whose principles, teachings and precepts can be adapted to every age, every hour, every circumstance. We don't need a change. We need to stick to the old-fashioned way of doing things. After all, if we change with the tide of time, where is there a stopping point? Where is there a place to say, "We go this far and no farther"? It's like some people say, "I believe some parts of the Bible." Well, which parts? If we accept only parts of the Scriptures as verbally inspired, which parts are we going to accept? Therefore, I declare unto you that we should and we do accept the entirety of the Bible. Book by book, chapter by chapter, verse by verse, line by line, word by word, syllable by syllable, we accept the inspiration of the Scriptures. We have reached the time when preachers ought to call their people back to the Book and back to God's way of doing things.

Divine Order

If you study carefully the first few chapters of the book of Acts, you will discover that, first of all, the *prayers* went up.

That's what we need in this hour. We will never have the power of God until we learn to pray. The *power* came down. The *people* went out. The *prospects* came in. The *persecution* broke out. But by then, multitudes were added to the church.

I'm convinced that, if we would have a great wave of persecution against the church in the twentieth century, it would drive us to our knees. There's no challenge anymore. The average church member takes the church for granted. The average nonchurch member takes the church for granted. I wonder if it wouldn't be good for us if a wave of persecution would break out against us. The church experienced its greatest period of growth when it was being persecuted.

It's altogether too easy for us to be in church. I firmly and frankly believe the reason a lot of people are not in church is that it's too easy. It's too convenient to be in church. It's too easy to join a church and be a part of a church anymore. God, help us to come back to the ancient path and to the Acts way and the Bible way and God's way of church and Sunday school building. That way is by our going out in the power of the Holy Spirit and, saturated with prayer, visiting and witnessing and sharing and inviting and enlisting others to come and hear the Word of God. Does not the Bible say that faith cometh by hearing and hearing by the Word of God?

So we're living in a world of change—governmental changes, educational changes, social changes, economic changes, cultural changes, religious changes—but thanks be unto God . . .

Jesus Christ Never Changes

My text says, "Jesus Christ the same yesterday, and to day, and for ever." I'm happy to report to you that the *power* of Jesus Christ has not diminished. He is no less powerful tonight than He was long ago when He spoke and the heavens came into existence, when He created the heaven and the earth, and made all animal life and plant life and human life to dwell thereon.

Jesus Christ is the same in His *love*. Here is a love wherewith He has loved us that cannot be measured. The Bible says, "For God so loved the world, that he gave his only begotten Son, that whosoever believeth in him should not perish, but have everlasting life." "Herein is love, not that we loved God, but that he loved us, and sent his Son to be the propitiation [or mercy seat] for our sins." Jesus Christ loves us as much as He loved those disciples who walked with Him along the streets of Jerusalem and up and down the shores of Lake Galilee. That love has not diminished. That love has not changed. "Jesus Christ the same yesterday, and to day, and for ever" in His love toward us.

Jesus Christ has not changed in His *mercy*. He has just as much mercy as ever. It is an inexhaustible supply. His mercy cannot be diminished, cannot be exhausted. He is mercy personified. He is the same in His mercy.

He is the same in His *grace*. The grace of God is just as sweet and powerful to us today as it was to the Christians in the first century. God said to the Apostle Paul, "My grace is sufficient for thee"; He says the same thing to us.

Jesus Christ is the same in His *power of preservation*. We are preserved by the same power that the early disciples were preserved by. There is no change. He is just as willing to save now as ever. If we were to live upon this earth a million years, He would still be the same, because we have a written guarantee that Jesus Christ never, never changes. He is the same yesterday and today and forever.

Looking Back

Some of you can remember back when the days of revival were on. Hundreds of people were saved. People really made something out of going to church. It was really an experience to sit down, open the Book of God, hear the man of God, sing the songs of Zion and worship Christ. God hasn't changed.

Jesus Christ hasn't changed. The Bible hasn't changed. So that leaves the change within us. The same supply of love and mercy and grace that's always been, is now, if we would but learn by faith how to tap the source and really believe God. We say that we believe God. We say that we have faith in God. But ladies and gentlemen, if we really believe God, there would be some changes in our lives. If we really believe that Jesus Christ is coming soon, there would be some changes in our way of operation. If we really believe that one day born-again believers, saved people, Christians are going to stand at the bema—the judgment seat of Christ—to give an account of our deeds upon the earth, wouldn't there be some changes in our lives? If we knew that there was being recorded everything we said, don't you think we would leave off some of the things we say? If we knew that there was a record made of the very intents and thoughts of our hearts, don't you really believe we would think differently?

O beloved, there is a record being made. God is the great Bookkeeper and Recorder. There are no flaws in His system. He is writing in a Book of Remembrance. Paul says, "So then every one of us shall give account of himself to God." God help us to begin to change and alter and rectify things in our lives that ought not to be there.

If we're going to stay within the framework of the Bible, we must adopt biblical principles by which we live. Many Christians think they've done God a favor when they come to church. Just what is Christianity and the Christian life to a whole lot of people? Coming to church on Sunday— that's it. It doesn't go beyond that. Many church members have no idea what Christian living really is because the only time they are really exposed to it, the only time there's evidence of it, is while they are in church. But something is wrong with one's Christianity when it can't go with him on the job and in the home and on the street and in the marketplace.

God help us to see that we're serving a never-changing

Christ. "Jesus Christ the same yesterday, and to day, and for ever."

Three questions we now ask:

1. Where Was Christ Yesterday?

In the yesterday of eternity, He was in the bosom of the Father.

"In the beginning was the Word, and the Word was with God, and the Word was God, The same was in the beginning with God. . . . And the Word was made flesh, and dwelt among us, (and we beheld his glory, the glory as of the only begotten of the Father,) full of grace and truth."—John 1:1,2,14.

In verse 18 of that same chapter Jesus said, "No man hath seen God at any time; the only begotten Son, which is in the bosom of the Father, he hath declared him."

Where was Jesus yesterday? In the yesterday of eternity He was in the bosom of the Father. In the beginning was the Word, the *logos*. There was never a time when Jesus Christ did not exist. There was never a time when there was not a second person of the Trinity. There was never a time when there was not that eternal *logos*—that eternal Word—in the beginning with God. So Jesus, in the yesterday of eternity, was in the bosom of the Father.

In the yesterday of time, He was upon the earth. The very first mention of Christ coming to the earth is found in Genesis 3:15, where God says there would be "a seed of the woman." For a long time that bothered the rabbis, until they read in the book of Isaiah, "Therefore the Lord himself shall give you a sign; Behold, a virgin shall conceive, and bear a son, and shall call his name Immanuel" (7:14), which, being interpreted, is, God with us.

So the very first mention of the Messiah, the Lord Jesus, coming to the earth in the flesh is in Genesis 3:15; and the enmity that is between the seed of the serpent and the Seed of the woman has been waging in unseen conflict from that day until this. The heel of the Seed of the woman, the Messiah, was bruised on the cross; but thanks be unto God, the story does not end there, for there will be a bruising of the head of Satan at the return of Christ.

They waited in anticipation for the fulfillment of the Scripture. And one day an angel came down to a virgin espoused to Joseph whose name was Mary and said unto her, 'That which is born of thee of the Holy Ghost overshadowing thee shall be called the Son of God.' So "when the fulness of the time was come, God sent forth his Son, made of a woman, made under the law" (Gal. 4:4)—and Jesus came into the world in the flesh. She brought forth her firstborn Son, wrapped Him in swaddling clothes and laid Him in a manger.

That's where Jesus was in the yesterday of time. He became man. He took upon Himself the likeness of sinful flesh. He lived upon the earth as a man. He breathed as a man. He ate as a man. He slept as a man. Yet at the same wonderful time, He was God— just as much God as though He had never been man, and just as much man as though He had not been God.

Jesus Christ in the yesterday of time walked upon the face of the earth, despised and rejected of men, a man of sorrows and acquainted with grief.

One day they arrested Him. They tried Him in a mock, unfair, unjust trial. Then they led Him away to Golgotha's hill, and there they crucified Him. That is where He was in the yesterday of time.

2. Where Is Christ Today?

At the right hand of God making intercession for us. There is not one pain that passes through your body that He does not feel. There is not one tear that wets your cheek that He is not aware of. There is not one sleepless night, not one aching in your heart, not one moment of temptation in your life that He does not know about. "For we have not an high

priest which cannot be touched with the feeling of our infir-
mities; but was in all points tempted like as we are, yet
without sin." Yes, my friend, Jesus knows all about your sorrows, your heartaches, your burdens, your problems, your
cares, your difficulties, your misgivings, your misunder-
standings, because He is at the right hand of God making
intercession for you.

It's a grand and glorious thought to know that anytime we
miss the mark, anytime we fumble the ball, anytime we stub
our spiritual toe, anytime we fall in the race, we don't have
to stay down. We may fall down or get knocked down, but
we don't have to stay down because the moment we look by
faith to Him, He intercedes and pleads our cause to the
Father.

Where is He today? At the right hand of God, yet in the
person of the Holy Spirit, He is right there in your heart. That
is one of the amazing things about our relationship to Christ.
In the person of the blessed Holy Spirit, He is in our midst,
in our hearts. The Spirit Himself beareth witness with our
spirit that we are the sons of God. The Holy Spirit is in every
believer. The moment a person is saved, the moment he believes, the Holy Spirit takes up His abode in that life.

Where is Jesus tonight? Though He is positionally and
majestically seated at the right hand of God, in the person
of the Holy Spirit, He is in your heart and mine.

3. Where Will Jesus Be in the
Tomorrows of Forever?

Until He comes again, He will be at the right hand of God.
Trouble, turmoil, strife, difficulty, apostasy, indifference—
surely all of which things point to the soon coming of our
Lord. Is something glorious about to take place? Though we
do not know the time nor the hour, we wait with expectancy,
with fond hope, with prayer, with patience, for Jesus Christ
to come. When He comes, He will rapture away those who
are looking for Him.

Oh, that will be the breaking of a new day for the believer! Then there shall be a great period of consternation and suffering upon the earth that the Bible calls the Great Tribulation. We believe that period to be the last week of Daniel's seventy weeks. Seven years long, and as that awesome week comes to a close, the forces of unrighteousness and the armies of the nations of the earth will gather against Jerusalem.

I used to hear the late Dr. Frank Norris preach on Zechariah 14. He could take that verse and go all the way back in world history and go all the way forward into future prophecy and bring together a great surrounding around the city of Jerusalem. And that is what is happening now. Down through the Mediterranean is where this show is, where the action will take place. The armies and navies of the various countries of the world will gather there. God says, "I will gather them together against Jerusalem for to battle."

But wait! When the awesome blow is about to be made, Jesus, in the brightness of His coming in the revelation glory with His saints, shall forever destroy the powers of Satan and the underworld.

Where will Jesus be in the tomorrows of forever and for eternity? Coming from the sky to rapture His own, to take us away to enjoy that wonderful honeymoon, the marriage supper of the Lamb, then to come back with Him to establish His kingdom upon the earth. We indeed believe in the pretribulation and premillennial coming of Christ. God is getting His people ready all over the world. If only we could be in the midst of a great revival—an old-time, old-fashioned, Holy Ghost, Heaven-sent revival—when He comes.

If I didn't believe it, I'd be of all men most miserable. I believe the same Gospel that Paul preached on Mars' Hill. I believe the same Gospel that Peter preached on the day of Pentecost. I believe the same Gospel that our forefathers have preached through the years. It's good enough to live by, and it's good enough to die by.

"Jesus Christ the same yesterday, and to day, and for ever."

9

THE BIBLE

and the Cross

"But God forbid that I should glory, save in the cross of our Lord Jesus Christ, by whom the world is crucified unto me, and I unto the world."—Gal. 6:14.

Someone said to the prince of preachers, Charles Haddon Spurgeon, "Mr. Spurgeon, all your sermons sound alike," to which he answered, without apology, "Yes, I take a text anywhere in the Bible and make a beeline for the cross." It is said that ninety-five percent of Spurgeon's sermons centered about the cross.

The cross is the heart of the Gospel, the sum and summation of all that God has done for man and all that man has done against God. On the cross while He was dying, the Son of God paid the supreme price, bearing our sins in His own body on the tree that we, being dead to sin, should live unto righteousness.

Symbol of Christianity

The cross is the symbol of Christianity. This is deep, and this is meaningful. We do not have as a symbol of our faith a halo. We do not have the statue of a bull. We do not have a sword. We do not have a spear. We do not have a half-moon. The symbol of Christianity is the cross. And the hallmark of the church is the cross.

Who can scale the majestic heights of the cross? Who can fathom its measureless depths? Who can speak of its awful shame? Who can sing of its wonderful glory? The cross reveals the dedication of Christ's life, the measure of His sacrifice. The cross reveals the dimension of God's love. How much does God love a sinful world? We have the answer in John 3:16, "For God so loved the world, that he gave his only begotten Son, that whosoever believeth in him should not perish, but have everlasting life."

If you want to know the degree of God's love for you, take a second look at the cross. There on the cross is the epitome, the zenith, the full measure of God's love for mankind. The cross reveals the depth of man's sin. How sinful is a race? How stooped in sin is a people who would nail an innocent Man to a cross and crucify Him in open, unapologetic shame! Sam Jones, the circuit-riding Methodist preacher, once said, "The cross is a symbol of God's heartbreak over a world gone astray."

The Cross Prominent in the Old Testament

The cross is prominent in the Old Testament.

The cross is seen in the Garden of Eden in the lamb slain to cover the nakedness of our first parents, Adam and Eve.

The cross is seen in the sacrifice offered by Abel, when men worshiped and called upon the name of the Lord.

The cross is seen in Abraham's life. When he built an altar, it was a symbol of the cross.

The cross is seen in the lamb caught in the thicket on

Mount Moriah as a substitute for Isaac.

The cross is seen on the night when Israel made her exodus out of the land of darkness and slavery and sin—the land of Egypt.

The cross is seen in the offerings of the Levitical priesthood in the Tabernacle in yonder wilderness.

The Cross Central in the New Testament

The cross is central in the New Testament.

The cross was the message of John the Baptist from the Jordan River. "Behold the Lamb of God, which taketh away the sin of the world."

The cross was the message of Peter, who stood with holy boldness on the day of Pentecost and preached Christ crucified and risen from the grave.

The cross was the message of Paul as he traveled across Asia and Europe. As he stood in the midst of Mars' Hill and proclaimed the Gospel of redeeming grace, his message was the cross.

The cross was the message of Jesus Christ Himself in the upper room at the Last Supper. Jesus said to His disciples about Himself, "This is my blood which is shed for many for the remission of sins."

Remember the Cross

Here's an interesting note in the Gospel. The one thing that Jesus asked us to remember was not His virgin birth, though we remember with reverence how the Holy Spirit came upon Mary and that which was conceived in her was born of the Holy Ghost. He asked us not to remember His sermon on the mount, though we remember it with glad hearts, for this is the law of His kingdom—a law of righteousness and love. He asked not for us to remember His majestic glory on the Mount of Transfiguration when He was transfigured and His face was like the brightness of the noonday sun. But beloved,

Jesus asked us to remember His death on the cross—"This do in remembrance of me." So the pattern of the New Testament is to come together around the communion cup and remember Jesus, remember His dying on the cross for our sins.

Supreme Sacrifice for Sin

He does not save by His supernatural birth, nor by His beautiful life, nor by His divine teachings, nor by His magnificent miracles. Jesus Christ saves by His sacrificial, substitutionary death on the cross. For without the shedding of blood, there is no remission of sin. If there had been no cross, there would be no sacrifice for sin. I trace the sacrificial animals from Adam through Abel and Aaron and right on down to the cross.

I remember so vividly when attending seminary the teaching of Dr. Louis Entzminger. God bless his memory! We owe a great debt to men like him. I shall never forget when he talked about the sacrifice. He spoke of the Levitical priesthood. He spoke of all the lambs of sacrifice from Adam onward. And he would always conclude by saying, "Young men, let me remind you that God was never, but never fully satisfied with the Levitical priesthood and all of its blood and all of its sufferings." And dear Dr. Entzminger would stand upon his tiptoes and say, "But when His Son died on the cross, it seems to me that God smelled the odor of the burning sacrifice and said, 'Forever My soul is satisfied.'"

This is the supreme sacrifice for sin.

I repeat: If there had been no cross, there would have been no sacrifice for sin. If there had been no cross, there would be no pardon, no peace, no reconciliation, no justification, no sanctification. There would be no remission of sin, no regeneration, no redemption and no forgiveness. Paul writes, "In whom we have redemption through his blood, even the forgiveness of sins."

This is what the cross is all about. And, beloved, the cross was no afterthought with God. It was no last resort. It was not as though God tried everything else and failed. Then He sent His Son to die on Calvary's cross. Oh, no! The cross was *prearranged* by God's wisdom, *preordained* by God's grace, and *prescheduled* by God's mercy. The eyes of all the patriarchs and prophets and priests were focused upon the cross. Jesus said, 'Abraham saw my day, and was glad.' Every book in the Old Testament anticipates the cross. According to Revelation 13:8, Jesus was the Lamb of God slain in the mind of God before the foundation of the world. Jesus Himself said, "For this cause came I into the world."

Christ and the Cross

Consider Jesus and the cross. Jesus Christ was born in Bethlehem's manger under the shadow of the cross. Jesus played in the streets of Nazareth under the shadow of the cross. Jesus attended the synagogues in His hometown under the shadow of the cross. Jesus worked in Joseph's carpenter shop under the shadow of the cross. Jesus was baptized in the Jordan River under the shadow of the cross. Jesus was tempted in the wilderness by the Devil under the shadow of the cross.

Jesus attended the wedding in Cana of Galilee under the shadow of the cross. Jesus sailed the Sea of Tiberias under the shadow of the cross. Jesus performed miracles in His ministry under the shadow of the cross. Jesus taught in the Temple in Jerusalem under the shadow of the cross. Jesus ate the last passover meal in the upper chamber under the shadow of the cross.

Then an amazing thing happened. The cross became a reality. The shadow became the substance. John says, "And he bearing his cross went forth into a place called the place of a skull, which is called in the Hebrew Golgotha." Luke says, "And when they were come to a place called Calvary, there they crucified him."

Oh, the wonder of the cross! No wonder Paul said, "God

forbid that I should glory, save in the cross of our Lord Jesus
Christ." No wonder we sing,

> **When I survey the wondrous cross,**
> **On which the Prince of glory died,**
> **My richest gain I count but loss,**
> **And pour contempt on all my pride.**
>
> **Were the whole realm of nature mine,**
> **That were a present far too small;**
> **Love so amazing, so divine,**
> **Demands my soul, my life, my all.**

No wonder we sing,

At the cross, at the cross where I first saw the light,
And the burden of my heart rolled away,
It was there by faith I received my sight,
And now I am happy all the day!

Is it any wonder we sang a moment ago,

> **On a hill far away stood an old rugged cross,**
> **The emblem of suff'ring and shame;**
> **And I love that old cross where the dearest and best**
> **For a world of lost sinners was slain.**

At the Cross

Our prayer ought to be in the words of that song, "Jesus,
keep me near the cross"; for, beloved, the cross is the central point, the focal point of our redemption. On the cross
He paid the price for our sins. Mount Sinai had its burning
bush, but it's not to be compared to the flaming sacrifice on
Calvary's tree. Mount Horeb had its Ten Commandments,
but they are not to be compared to Calvary's law of love.
Mount Moriah had its lamb caught in a thicket, but it's not
to be compared to Calvary's Lamb for sinners slain.

The cross is the intersection where God and man meet.
The cross is the cornerstone of man's redemption. The cross
is the watchtower of God's grace. The cross is the core of
our Christian faith. Without the cross, we would have no

message. Without the cross, we would have no experience of salvation. Without the cross, we would have no blessed hope.

The cross is a fact of history. One hundred and seventy-five times His death is mentioned in the New Testament. In the last twenty-four hours of our Lord's life, thirty-two prophecies were fulfilled. Twenty-five of the eighty-nine chapters of the four gospel accounts speak of His death. It is a matter of record that around the year 30 A.D., Christ of Nazareth was crucified under Pontius Pilate; and the world—a world of sin, sorrow and shame—is indebted to Christ for the price He paid on Calvary's tree.

What do we see when we look at the cross? The Romans saw another helpless victim of imperial tyranny. The Greeks saw another blight on their culture and on the history of civilization. The Jews saw another false messiah dying. One of the thieves who was crucified with Him saw another criminal like himself dying for his sins. The other thief saw the Just dying for the unjust. God saw His Son dying for the sins of the world. We see Christ, our Saviour, bearing our sins in His own body on that cruel cross.

What really took place at the cross anyway? At the cross, Christ put away sin by the sacrifice of Himself.

At the cross, Christ passed through the valley of death.

At the cross, Christ canceled our stupendous debt that we owe to the law of God.

At the cross, Christ was wounded for our transgressions.

At the cross, Christ was bruised for our iniquities.

At the cross, the chastisement of our peace was upon Him.

At the cross, by His stripes we are healed.

At the cross, Christ reconciled a guilty world to a righteous God.

At the cross, Christ opened the prison door and set the captive free.

At the cross, Christ made the supreme sacrifice for sin.

At the cross, Christ condemned sin forever.

At the cross, Christ became our Substitute, dying in our stead.

At the cross, Christ tasted death for every man.

At the cross, God emptied Himself and died in open shame.

At the cross, God turned on His own Son and poured out the vials of His wrath upon Jesus that day.

At the cross, God darkened the sun and shook the earth.

At the cross, God laid on Christ the iniquity of us all.

At the cross, Christ was made sin that we might be made that righteousness of God in Him.

At the cross, love was spelled out in brilliant letters across a sky darkened with sin.

At the cross, the Lamb of God was slain without mercy at the hands of His enemies.

At the cross, Heaven's camera bent low to capture earth's saddest scene.

At the cross, the grace of God turned a great tragedy into a great triumph.

At the cross, all the sacrifices from Adam onward were terminated in one supreme sacrifice.

At the cross, all human suffering finds its refuge in the Saviour's wounds.

At the cross, Satan was disarmed, and sin met his Conqueror.

At the cross, the fires of Sinai were extinguished by the blood of Emmanuel.

At the cross, the death sentence was commuted to life eternal.

At the cross, the road to life eternal was paved, and the door of Heaven was forever opened.

At the cross, at the cross, I first saw the light, and the burden in my heart as an eleven-year-old boy rolled away.

A little old lady past eighty lay dying. The missionaries had come and won her to Christ. They had told her of the nail prints in His hands and the riven side. You see, a lot of people have a mistaken idea about Christ. They think He was nailed to the cross after He died; but not so. Jesus was nailed alive to the cross and lifted up to die an awful death. No wonder the sun refused to shine. No wonder God turned His back. No wonder the earth did quake with mighty power. For six long hours He was dying—dying for you and for me.

When the Catholic priest came into the community on his annual journey through the little village, someone told him that Sister So-and-so was at the point of death. Well, thinking he had the keys that opened Heaven and no one out of his parish could enter without his permission, he went over to this little, precious, godly woman and said, "I have come to grant you absolution."

She didn't know what that meant. She thought she had all that she needed. So she asked him, "Mister, what do you mean you have come to grant me; what did you say?"

He said, "Absolution."

She said, "Tell me, what does that mean?"

"Oh," he said in simple, plain language, "it means that I've come to forgive you of your sins."

She replied, "Mister, let me see your hands." She gazed at the hands of the priest, then said, "Mister, you are an imposter!"

"Oh," he said, "you don't understand. See my clerical robes? I have the authority of the church."

She said again, "Mister, you are a fake."

"But I don't understand. What do you mean?"

She said, "Mister, the Man who forgives me of my sin has nail prints in His hands."

The only thing that will be in Heaven that man put there will be the nail prints in His hands and the scar in His side. Didn't one of the prophets say, "Where did You receive these wounds?" They will still be showing. Jesus answered, "In the house of my friends."

Thank God for the nail prints in His hands! Paul tells us that He nailed to the tree all of the ordinances and the handwriting of the law that was contrary to us. Thank God for the nail-scarred hand!

Who Was at the Cross?

Who was at the cross that day? The gamblers were there. The soldiers were there. The spectators were there. His enemies were there. His friends were there. His mother was there. And, ladies and gentlemen, I feel, as you surely feel, we were there. The poet put it like this:

I see the crowd in Pilate's hall, I mark their wrathful mien;
Their shouts of "Crucify" appall with blasphemy between;
And of that shouting multitude, I feel that I am one;
And in that den of voices rude, I recognized my own.
'Twas I who shed the sacred blood, I nailed Him to the tree,
I crucified the Son of God, I joined the mockery.
Around the cross, the throng I see mocking the Sufferer's
**   groan;**
Yet still my voice, it seems to be as if I mocked alone.

It was my sins, your sins, that nailed Him to the cross. Can the cross be measured? No! Ten thousand times no! If all the sorrow from the creation till this moment were poured into one cup, it could not compare to the cup of sorrow on Calvary's hill. If all the floods—from Noah's to the mighty Missisippi last week—were brought together, they could not compare to the flood of grief that rolled over the soul of the Son of God. If all the fires from Sinai to San Francisco were put together in one burning inferno, it could not compare to the fire of God's judgment at the cross. If all the darkness from Egypt to New York's great blackout were concentrated into one cubicle of darkness, it could not compare to the darkness of Calvary. If all the books written from Job to the latest one off the press were combined into one volume, they could not tell the story of the cross. If all the paintings from Solomon to Picasso were hung in a gallery, they could not depict the anguish of the Son of God hanging on Calvary's cross.

Seven Last Words

No, the cross cannot be measured. It is unfathomable. It is immeasurable. It is unspeakable. Oh, it is so much that we cannot begin to touch the hem of the garment of the sufferings of the Saviour.

From the cross that day came seven last words from the Saviour: (1) a word of *forgiveness.* He prayed, "Father, forgive them; for they know not what they do"; (2) a word of *assurance.* To the dying thief He said, "To day shalt thou be with me in paradise"; (3) a word of *devotion.* Jesus said to His mother Mary, "Woman, behold thy Son," speaking of John the beloved apostle; and to John He said, "Son, behold thy mother"; (4) a word of *despair.* God turned His own back on His Son. God couldn't bear to look on that ugly spectacle, and loudly He must have cried from the anguish of soul, "My God, my God, why hast thou forsaken me?" A word of despair.

A man said to his pastor following his son's death in an accident, "Pastor, tell me, where was God when my son died in that accident?" The pastor wisely answered, "The same place He was when His Son died on the cross." "My God, my God, why hast thou forsaken me?"

(5) A word of *agony.* Jesus cried, "I thirst"; (6) a word of *victory.* "It is finished." In the Greek the word is *tetelestai—* "paid in full." When you get that note from the bank three years, four years, twenty years from now and it is stamped, "Paid in Full," the bank can never, never collect another dime from you. Why? *Tetelestai!* It is finished! The account is paid in full.

That's precisely what Christ did for us on the cross—paid the debt in full. It is finished.

(7) A word of *confidence.* Jesus cried, "Father, into thy hands I commend my spirit." Read carefully the words of

this poem, "The Cross Was His Own":

They borrowed a bed to lay His head when Christ the Lord came down.
They borrowed the ass in the mountain pass for Him to ride to town,
But the crown He wore and the cross He bore were His own.
He borrowed the bread when the crowd He fed on the grassy mountain side.
He borrowed the dish of broken fish with which He satisfied,
But the crown He wore and the cross He bore were His own.
He borrowed the ship in which to sit to teach the multitude.
He borrowed the nest in which to rest. He had never a home so rude,
But the crown He wore and the cross He bore were His own.
He borrowed a room on the way to the tomb, the passover lamb to eat.
They borrowed a cave for Him a grave. They borrowed the winding sheet,
But the crown He wore and the cross He bore were His own.
The thorns on His head were worn in my stead; for me the Saviour died.
For guilt of my sins the nails drove in, when Him they crucified.
Though the crown He wore and the cross He bore were His own, they rightly were mine.

In the city of London, in the geographical center is a charring cross. This actual cross stands high above the other buildings. Measurements from the outskirts of London are measured to the cross. Directions are given by the city and city officials and the policemen by the cross.

One day a little boy was lost. The bobby, or policeman, talked to him. He was so broken up, so disturbed, so distraught that the child couldn't even given them his address. He could hardly give them his name. But in a little while he regained his composure. Looking up at the policeman, he said, "Mister, if you'll show me the cross, I can find my way home."

That's my message. I've shown you the cross; now find your way Home.

**I must needs go Home by the way of the cross,
There's no other way but this;
I shall ne'er get sight of the Gates of Light,
If the way of the cross I miss.**

It's all in the Book—the Bible and the cross!

10

THE BIBLE

and Religion

"Then Paul stood in the midst of Mars' hill, and said, Ye men of Athens, I perceive that in all things ye are too superstitious. For as I passed by, and beheld your devotions, I found an altar with this inscription, TO THE UNKNOWN GOD. Whom therefore ye ignorantly worship, him declare I unto you."—Acts 17:22,23.

These two verses form a part of the great sermon that the Apostle Paul delivered from Mars' Hill. The city of Athens, Greece, was at that time the intellectual capital of the world. It was not only a city of intellectuals, but it was a city of commerce and a city of trade. Even from the city of Rome, families would send their young men to be educated in Athens. The great systems of philosophy, two of which are mentioned in Acts 17, Epicureans and the Stoics, were well known in Athens. Earlier there were other philosophers such as Plato,

Socrates and Aristotle, whose systems of philosophy sprang up in Athens.

So Paul was not speaking to an ordinary group of people. He was speaking to men of unusual wisdom, yet Paul did not "water down" his message. Paul spoke with holy boldness concerning God, His creation, His Son, the Lord Jesus Christ, His plan and program of salvation for all men, giving special emphasis to the resurrection of Christ from the dead.

The Greeks believed in immortality. They believed that, when a man died, his soul would continue on "somewhere," perhaps to join in some mass ectoplasm in another world; but they did not believe in the bodily resurrection of the individual. Thus Paul emphasizes and reemphasizes the resurrection by pointing to the fact that Jesus Christ had been raised from the dead.

Paul was in the midst of a people who were not only intellectually on the top shelf, but these people were very religious.

The Riddle of Religion

I begin my message with a riddle. What is worldwide in scope, something that almost everybody has in some form or another, and is used by millions as a substitute for the real thing? If you answered "religion," you're correct. Indeed, religion is worldwide in scope. Millions of people subscribe to some doctrine, some belief, some system of religion somewhere in the world, and the sad and tragic note in it all is this: they are using religion as a substitute for the real thing.

One of the most difficult things about religion is its definition. How would you define religion? Someone has suggested that there have been perhaps ten thousand definitions given. Webster, with whom most of us are familiar, defines religion as follows: "The service and adoration of God or of a god as expressed in forms of worship."

There are in the world eleven major religions: Hinduism,

Buddhism, Confucianism, Mohammedanism, Sikhism, Taoism, Shintoism, Zoroastrianism, Jainism, Judaism and Christianity. Of these eleven, eight are older than Christianity. Two have come into existence since the birth of Christ—Sikhism and Mohammedanism. All of the other eight were already existing when Christ was born.

Christianity

Christianity is by no means the oldest religion in the world, but the difference between Christianity and all other religions is Christ, and this difference is as wide as eternity. Jesus Christ makes Christianity a way of life with eternal dimensions. All other religions say in essence, "Do and Live." Christianity says, "Live and Do."

Under consideration is one of the most serious problems in all the world—the problem of religion. Someone has said that man is incurably religious. I think this is borne out by the fact that, of the more than four billion people who populate the earth, some three billion adhere to some kind of religion. In the realm of Christianity, there are some one billion followers. That does not mean one billion born-again believers, because many are counted in the realm of Christianity who have never had a personal experience with Christ, and the Bible says, "Except a man be born again, he cannot enter into the kingdom of heaven."

What does it mean to be a Christian? It means to have Christ living within. A Christian is a "Christ one"—one who has passed from death unto life, one who has had that personal encounter that we call the new birth. To Nicodemus, Jesus said, "Ye must be born again."

Religion and God

Religion does not save, does not satisfy, does not secure. Religion is only a passing fancy of the mind. Most anybody in some form or another can be religious. Religion only temporarily pacifies the insatiable appetite that man has to identify himself with some mystic power beyond his own means.

In the words that I read you from the lips of the Apostle Paul, he said to the Athenians, "I perceive that in all things ye are too superstitious." As Paul made his way to the top of Mars' Hill, he passed no less than twelve altars. Athens was known for its gods and goddesses. In fact, someone went so far as to say, "You could as soon meet a god in Athens as you could a man." This city was given over wholly to idolatry, to idol worship. When Paul saw these twelve altars to twelve different gods, he observed on one of those altars this inscription: "TO THE UNKNOWN GOD." Paul says. 'I will declare unto you the unknown God.'

Why do you suppose the Athenians had an altar with that inscription? I believe they wanted to make sure that, if there were another god whom they had not known nor identified, he would be included in the inscription. Paul declares that, because he is to them unknown, they are worshiping him in ignorance. "Him declare I unto you," said Paul.

Man must know God before he can be saved. These people were offering their sacrifices and making their prayers to a God unknown to them. I repeat, man must know God before he can be saved, and man must know God by experience, not by explanation.

Who Is God?

I pose for you this question: Who can explain God? In Romans 11:33-36 Paul writes words like these:

"O the depth of the riches both of the wisdom and knowledge of God! how unsearchable are his judgments, and his ways past finding out! For who hath known the mind of the Lord? or who hath been his counsellor? Or who hath first given to him, and it shall be recompensed unto him again? For of him, and through him, and to him, are all things: to whom be glory for ever. Amen."

There is not a mind so keen, there is not a brain so brilliant that can reach through the intellect, the wisdom, might and knowledge of God. The sinner cannot know God through education. If he could, just how intelligent would a man have to be? The sinner cannot know God by science. If he could, what scientific formula would he use? The sinner cannot know God by religion. If he could, just what religion would he choose? The only way a sinner can know God is through His Son, the Lord Jesus Christ. Jesus said, "I am the way, the truth, and the life: no man cometh unto the Father, but by me." Paul supports this truth in the book of Hebrews when he writes:

"God, who at sundry times and in divers manners spake in time past unto the fathers by the prophets, Hath in these last days spoken unto us by his Son, whom he hath appointed heir of all things, by whom also he made the worlds; Who being the brightness of his glory, and the express image of his person, and upholding all things by the word of his power, when he had by himself purged our sins, sat down on the right hand of the Majesty on high."— Heb. 1:1-3.

The Way to God

God has always had only one way of approach to His throne, and that is through Jesus Christ. No man can ever reach the Father unless he goes through the Son. So religion is not the answer. The Bible declares in I Timothy 2:5, "For there is one God, and one mediator between God and men, the man Christ Jesus."

Our God is the Creator of heaven and earth and all that is therein. Our God is the possessor of all things. It is so declared in Psalm 24:1: "The earth is the Lord's, and the fulness thereof; the world, and they that dwell therein."

We speak often about "my property," "my house," "my land," "my ranch," "my farm," "my cows," "my bank account" and "my clothes." But, beloved, it all belongs to God.

He has only put us on a lend-lease basis. In His mercy and love, God has entrusted us as faithful stewards, those who look over the affairs of others. So that car that you drive is not your own. "But, pastor, I've got the title to it." So what? It belongs to God. The house you're living in is not yours. "But I just made the last payment last week." That's all right; it still doesn't belong to you. You see, one of these days, and maybe without a moment's notice, you and I may be wiped out. Mourners will pass by and say, "Well, he sure looks natural. Wasn't he a nice fellow?" (Isn't it strange how, after people die, almost everyone says something good about them? Even a sorry preacher becomes a good man after he's dead!) In just a few short days someone else will be jingling your keys, driving your car, sleeping in your bed and wearing your clothes. We will leave it all.

What I'm trying to say is—away with the philosophy that "this is mine." No, it's God's! God has just trusted you with it, and if you don't use it properly, He will take it away from you.

Where Does God Dwell?

God does not dwell in pagan temples. Go to the most magnificent cathedral in the world; God is not dwelling in those kinds of temples. It has been our privilege to stand in the Dome of the Rock Mosque in Jerusalem—a magnificent building. We have stood in St. Peter's Cathedral in Rome—a beautiful building, costing in the hundreds of millions of dollars. But God doesn't dwell in stone and brick and mortar. He dwells in human flesh—in your life and mine—in the person of the Holy Spirit. No need to go and bow down before a wooden idol or a stone idol or a golden idol. God is not there. He dwells within the heart and life of every born-again believer. The Bible says, "If any man hath not the Spirit of Christ, he is none of his." The way some of us live and the way we treat God and the way we treat God's program and the church and God's Bible and God's plan, sometimes it makes me wonder if God is dwelling within. God help us not to assume that, just because we've joined the church or signed a card or "gone forward," we're saved. It's one thing to be a church member; it's another thing to know Christ as your Saviour.

Our God has guided the history of nations throughout all time. I read in Isaiah 40 that all nations are like a drop in the bucket to Him. He is the great Sovereign of the universe.

There is a legend that the Emperor Julian, an unbeliever, an agnostic, was making light of Christ. He said to one of his servants, "What do you suppose the carpenter's son is doing now?" The servant wisely answered, "He's probably hewing out wood for your casket." God is ruling in the world.

God is still on His throne.
He will take care of His own.
His promises are true.
He will see you right through.
God is still on His throne.

Our God is omnipotent—that is, He is all-powerful. Nothing is too hard for Him. Our God is omniscient—that is, He knows everything. Nothing is hidden from Him. He knows the secret thoughts and intents of the heart.

Even the Bible itself testifies,

"For the word of God is quick, and powerful, and sharper than any twoedged sword, piercing even to the dividing asunder of soul and spirit, and of the joints and marrow, and is a discerner of the thoughts and intents of the heart."—Heb. 4:12.

God knows your Social Security number. He knows your telephone number, your zip code, your area code, your street number, your employment number, your wedding number. God knows *everything.* There's nothing hidden from Him. He's omniscient. He knows it all. God is omnipresent. He is everywhere. I read in Psalm 139:7-10:

"Whither shall I go from thy spirit? or whither shall I flee

from thy presence? If I ascend up into heaven, thou art there: if I make my bed in hell, behold, thou art there. If I take the wings of the morning, and dwell in the uttermost parts of the sea; Even there shall thy hand lead me, and thy right hand shall hold me."

A God of Salvation

Our God is the God of salvation. I read in Psalm 3:8, "Salvation belongeth unto the Lord." I read in Psalm 68:20, "He that is our God is the God of salvation." When Jesus Christ was born in Bethlehem in the long ago, the angel instructed His mother and foster father Joseph to name Him Jesus. Why? Because "he shall save his people from their sins." The word "Jesus" comes from two words—*Jehovah-hoshea*—"the God of salvation." Thanks be unto God! Our Saviour is named Jesus, the God of salvation.

You might ask, "What is the difference between religion and salvation?" Religion is an experience with a mystical idea, while salvation is an experience with a mighty Person.

"Neither is there salvation in any other, for there is none other name under heaven given among men whereby we must be saved."

"He that believeth on him is not condemned: but he that believeth not is condemned already, because he hath not believed on the name of the only begotten Son of God."

"He that believeth on the Son hath everlasting life: and he that believeth not the Son shall not see life, but the wrath of God abideth on him."

"He that heareth my word, and believeth on him that sent me, hath everlasting life, and shall not come into condemnation; but is passed from death unto life."

Religion is an experience which requires only a new thought. Salvation is an experience which requires a new birth. To Nicodemus, Jesus said, "Ye must be born again."

Religion is an experience which takes place in the head. Salvation is an experience that takes place in the heart. "For with the heart man believeth unto righteousness, and with the mouth confession is made unto salvation." Salvation is a heart matter. Something must happen in the heart. There must be a regeneration of the heart in order for a man to be saved.

Religion is an experience that is brought about by good works. Salvation is an experience that is brought about by God's grace. Paul declares in Ephesians 2:8,9, "For by grace are ye saved through faith; and that not of yourselves: it is the gift of God: Not of works, lest any man should boast."

Religion is an experience that involves receiving a creed. Salvation is an experience that involves receiving Christ. In John 1:11,12 we read, "He came unto his own, and his own received him not. But as many as received him, to them gave he power to become the sons of God, even to them that believe on his name."

Religion is external. Salvation is internal.

Religion is transferable. Salvation is nontransferable.

Religion is temporary. Salvation is permanent.

Religion is earthly. Salvation is heavenly.

Religion is cheap. Religion is a counterfeit. Salvation is the real thing.

Religion is endured. Salvation is enjoyed!

 THE BIBLE

and the Eternal Security of the Believer

"For the which cause I also suffer these things: nevertheless I am not ashamed: for I know whom I have believed, and am persuaded that he is able to keep that which I have committed unto him against that day."—II Tim. 1:12.

There is a passage of Scripture in the Old Testament, Ecclesiastes 3:14, that I would also share with you right at the beginning of the message:

"I know that, whatsoever God doeth, it shall be for ever: nothing can be put to it, nor any thing taken from it: and God doeth it, that men should fear before him."

There has always been a question in the minds of some

people concerning the perseverance of the saints. We commonly call it the eternal security of the believer. The basic question is: Can a truly born-again believer ever be lost? Can a child of God, born into the family of God, regenerated by the power of God, ever lose his salvation? It is the purpose of this message to set forth from the Scripture the answer to this age-old question.

Before answering the basic question, there are four things that we should establish. First, we establish that

"Salvation Belongeth Unto the Lord"

So says Psalm 3:8. In Ephesians 2:8,9 we read, "For by grace are ye saved through faith; and that not of yourselves: it is the gift of God: Not of works, lest any man should boast." And in Titus 3:5, "Not by works of righteousness which we have done, but according to his mercy he saved us...."

We establish, then, from the Word of God that salvation is not of man, but is of the Lord.

Second, we establish

The Difference Between True Believers and Mere Professors of Religion

There are those who profess Christ but do not possess Him. It is impossible for one to judge another. First Samuel 16:7 says that "man looketh on the outward appearance, but the Lord looketh on the heart." What you are on the outside may be altogether different from what you are on the inside. As has often been said, we cannot judge a book by its cover. What we set forth in our lives on the outside sometimes is far removed from that which is on the inside. So God and the individual are the only two who can know whether a man is truly born again. The Bible says some shall go even into eternity thinking they are saved, only to be confronted with the truth that they are lost. I support that statement by quoting Matthew 7:21-23:

"Not every one that saith unto me, Lord, Lord, shall enter

into the kingdom of heaven; but he that doeth the will of my Father which is in heaven. Many will say to me in that day, Lord, Lord, have we not prophesied in thy name? and in thy name have cast out devils? and in thy name done many wonderful works? And then will I profess unto them, I never knew you: depart from me, ye that work iniquity."

Does not Jesus make it plain that many people are going about with some sort of false hope that they are saved? I have never understood how a person can say he is saved and never go to church, never read his Bible, never serve Christ nor do one thing to show evidence of having been born into the family of God. I am not the judge. We have already stated only God and the individual know. But I reserve the right to have some serious doubts about those who have their names on the church rolls but know nothing of a personal encounter with the Holy Spirit.

I believe, if a man is saved, he will want to go to church. He will want to serve Christ. He will want to hear the Gospel. He will want to witness for Christ. If there is something in his heart, he will want to share it with someone else.

If your faith is not worth sharing, it's not worth having. If Christ is not worth sharing, He's not worth having. Jesus said, "By their fruits ye shall know them." Many simply professing to be Christians shall be astonished and amazed when they stand before God and hear the words, "Depart from me," although they have held this office or that office or done this or that in the framework of the church. The wheat and tares are growing together, and Jesus said it would be this way. There are professors and possessors, those who merely say, "I'm a Christian," and are not, and those who really possess salvation through Jesus Christ our Lord.

The third thing we need to establish is that

There Is a Difference Between Salvation and Rewards

A reward is something earned. The believer earns a reward

for service performed for Christ. Salvation is a present reality. Our rewards are a future possibility. There is a difference.

The fourth thing we need to establish is this:

What a Believer Can Lose

While we believe it is impossible for a believer to lose his
salvation, there are three things that a believer can lose:

1. A believer can lose the *peace* of God. Observe, there is
a difference between the peace *of* God and peace *with* God.
Peace with God relates to the individual's salvation. Paul
writes in Romans 5:1, "Therefore being justified by faith, we
have peace with God." Nothing can disturb that peace *with*
God. It relates to the individual's salvation. But the peace
of God relates to the individual's daily walk with Christ.

In Philippians 4:6, 7 Paul writes:

*"Be careful [anxious] for nothing; but in every thing by
prayer and supplication with thanksgiving let your re-
quests be made known unto God. And the peace of God,
which passeth all understanding, shall keep your hearts
and minds through Christ Jesus."*

I repeat: it is possible for a believer to lose the peace *of* God
from his heart, but not the peace *with* God.

2. It is possible for the believer to lose his *reward*. In I Corinthians 3:15 Paul writes: "If any man's work shall be
burned, he shall suffer loss: but he himself shall be saved;
yet so as by fire." It is possible, then, for a believer, who has
worked and labored for Christ and who has earned rewards
for Heaven, to lose the reward, though he himself shall be
saved.

3. It is possible for the believer to lose the *joy* of his salvation. A classic example is David. Remember that David
prayed in Psalm 51:12, "Restore unto me the joy of thy salvation." David did not pray, "Restore unto me thy salvation,"
but ". . . the joy of thy salvation." It is possible to lose the
joy of serving Christ, and that is true of many Christians

today. Many church members have lost the joy of serving Christ because of sin and selfishness. It is possible to lose the joy.

Can a Born-Again Believer Ever Be Lost?

Now the basic question: Can a born-again believer ever be lost? Never, because of the direct statement from Scripture concerning his security. Many, many passages relate to the security of the believer, but I share just two. In Philippians 1:6 Paul writes, "Being confident of this very thing, that he which hath begun a good work in you [is able to perform] will perform [Paul writes more emphatically] it until the day of Jesus Christ." ". . . *will perform*" means "to continue to perform." It is a continuous action verb—"will perform it until the day of Jesus Christ."

"Day of Christ" refers to the day when Christ shall appear, when Christ shall come to receive His own out of the world. So Paul is emphatically, unapologetically telling us that Jesus Christ is able to continue the work and will perform the work in the believer until the day He comes again.

The second Scripture is Romans 8:35-39. Paul asks the question:

"Who shall separate us from the love of Christ? shall tribulation, or distress, or persecution, or famine, or nakedness, or peril, or sword?. . . Nay, in all these things we are more than conquerors through him that loved us."

When Paul wrote that, he knew about the power of the Caesars. Paul had witnessed a part of the strongest segment of the Roman Empire. He knew ancient history. He knew about Nebuchadnezzar, about Tiglathpileser. He knew about the Caesars, so he wrote:

". . . we are more than conquerors through him that loved us. For I am persuaded, that neither death, nor life, nor angels, nor principalities, nor powers, nor things present, nor things to come, Nor height, nor depth, nor any other

creature, shall be able to separate us from the love of God, which is in Christ Jesus our Lord."

Paul says that no creature, no creature in Heaven or earth, is able to separate us from the love of Christ.

Once in Christ, in Christ forever.
Nothing from His love my soul can sever.

I've anchored my soul in the haven of rest,
I'll sail the wild seas no more;
The tempest may sweep o'er the wild stormy deep,
In Jesus I'm safe evermore.

Who shall separate us from the love of God? Nothing. No one in time or eternity can separate us from the love of God.

Eternal Life a Present Possession

The believer can never be lost because eternal life is a present possession. I've heard people pray, "And, Lord, save us all at last." Dear me! I'm glad I don't have a salvation that I'm wondering about. I'm glad I don't have to pray for God to save me sometime in the future, because He saved me when I was eleven years old. Why, then, would I ask Him to save me "at last" when I'm already saved? And I wouldn't thank an angel to come and stand on that piano and say, "You are saved," because I already know it. I have the witness of the Holy Spirit in my life. I know that I know that I know that I know that I'm saved.

Bless God! I wouldn't want any salvation I could not know about. I wouldn't give you a peanut hull for something I couldn't know about. Paul said, "I know whom I have believed."

Several words ought never be in the vocabulary of a Christian—*perhaps, maybe, hope so, if* and *peradventure.* We should underscore 'these things are written that ye might *know* ye have passed from death unto life.' "These things are written . . . ." I'm not basing my salvation on the way I feel. Honestly, sometimes the Devil makes me feel bad. My salvation is based upon the Word of God. I'm saved forever because God says I am. And if God says it, that settles it. So, I don't pray, "Lord, save us all at last in Heaven." Salvation is a present possession.

There are those who believe God gives us eternal life at death. No! We have eternal life *now*. Let me give you just a few passages of Scripture. In John 5:24 Jesus said,

"He that heareth my word, and believeth on him that sent me, hath [present tense] *everlasting life, and shall not come into condemnation* [or judgment]; *but is* [present tense] *passed from death unto life."*

Jesus said salvation is a present possession. In Romans 8:1 Paul writes: "There is therefore *now* [present], no condemnation to them which are in Christ Jesus, who walk not after the flesh, but after the Spirit." We are *now* free from condemnation. The Devil can never, but never, lay hold upon our eternal salvation. Now he is the prince of the power of the air, and in this age he is constantly accusing us. I can almost hear him pointing a finger down to Worth Baptist Church and saying, "Look at them! Why, don't you know that preacher lost his temper last week? Don't you know that family had a fight last week? Don't you know this man slipped and did something wrong last week?" The Devil is constantly accusing—BUT HE CAN'T GET US! If the Devil isn't after you, it could be a good sign he already has you; but with God's help, you can stay a step ahead of him.

I'm glad there is now no condemnation, no judgment, no eternal wrath, that all has been settled. I settled my account when I was eleven years old, but Jesus settled it almost two thousand years ago. On the cross He paid the debt. He answered every requirement. He bore in His own body my sins and your sins on the cross. He has suffered already the condemnation, the wrath, the fury, the anger, the judgment of God so that you and I will never have to suffer that. There is therefore now no condemnation to them that are in Christ Jesus. I'm in Him forever, and the Holy Spirit is in me.

In I John chapter 3, John writes: "Behold, what manner of love the Father hath bestowed upon us, that we should be called the sons of God." Amazing! We are called the "sons of God." Then John goes on to say, "Beloved, now [not next year, not next millennium, not in the future, not in eternity, but NOW] are we the sons of God, and it doth not yet appear what we shall be: but we know that, when he shall appear, we shall be like him; for we shall see him as he is." One day we will be exactly like Him.

It is said that someone once wrote Charles Haddon Spurgeon and said, "Please send me a picture of yourself and your autograph so I can put them in my book." Spurgeon wrote back, "Too bad you didn't wait a bit longer, because I'm going to be like Him, and you would have a far better picture of Charles Haddon Spurgeon."

When I anticipate, when I think of the glory and majesty that is going to be ours when we're like Him, it thrills my soul! Our God is rich. Our Father holds all of the wealth of the world in His hands. Why should we worry and be despondent? Our Father owns everything. Beloved, **now** are we the sons of God! Salvation is a present proposition.

> So near, so very near,
> Nearer I could not be,
> For in the person of His Son,
> I'm just as near as He.
>
> So dear, so very dear,
> Dearer I could not be,
> For the love wherewith He loves His Son,
> Such is His love for me.

Safe Because Placed in the Family of God

The believer can never be lost because he has been placed into the family of God by birth. We have a birthright and a birth certificate to prove it. The relationship between God and the Christian is a Father-son relationship. In Romans 8 we read, "For as many as are led by the Spirit of God, they are the sons of God." Then Paul goes on to write, "The Spirit itself beareth witness with our spirit, that we are the children of God: And if children then heirs; heirs of God, and joint-heirs with Christ."

Beloved, there is a Father-son relationship. He is our Father. We are His children because we have been born into His family. Jesus said to Nicodemus—and this applies to all men, "Except a man be born again, he cannot enter the kingdom of God." We enter the family of God by birth. Therefore, we are in His family by birthright.

In John 1:11,12 we read: "He came unto his own, and his own received him not. But as many as received him, to them gave he power to become the sons of God, even to them that believe on his name."

Then I read in Galatians 3:26: "For ye are all the children of God by faith in Christ Jesus."

Now a child can disrupt the fellowship that exists between himself and his father, but he can never, never rupture the relationship that exists between the two.

As a parent disciplines his child, so God disciplines His. I read in Hebrews 12:6: "For whom the Lord loveth he chasteneth, and scourgeth every son whom he receiveth." God will scourge, and God will chasten, but God will never cast out—John 6:37: "Him that cometh unto me, I will in no wise [under no circumstances, under no conditions] cast out."

When I was growing up, I did a lot of things that displeased my dad; and I have some things to show for it, too! I was whipped. We don't hear that word much anymore, but that's what a lot of us got—an old-fashioned "whooping." God too lays the lash upon His own children. My daddy used to whip or "whoop" me and scold me and punish me, but never one time did he ever cast me out of his family. Now he ran me out of the house several times because I was so cantankerous. When he said, "Get out of here," I got. But about supper time I was always back.

Ah, I like that family relationship. I could have changed my name, I could have disowned my family; but nothing in this world could ever change the relationship that I had with my dad. I am his son, and nothing can change that.

The same is true in our relationship to God. We are His sons, we are His family—and He will never, never cast us out.

We Are Hid With Christ

The believer can never be lost because his life is hid with Christ in God. Do you know what that says to me? If God ever banished us, He would have to banish Christ. If God ever cast us out, He would have to cast Christ out because we are with Christ in God—Colossians 3:3: "For ye are dead, and your life is hid with Christ in God."

In Revelation, chapter 2, there is a beautiful picture of Christ having in His hand the messengers of the various churches. I believe that this messenger would symbolize the church and all the believers, and the picture is Christ holding the believer in His hand. The word *hold* in the Greek is *criteo.* It has two uses—a genitive use and an accusative use. The genitive use means to hold a part of something. The accusative use means to hold completely and entirely.

Let's look at the genitive use. I'm holding this Bible in my hand. I might turn my head and someone come along and snatch that Book right out of my hand. That's the genitive use.

But in Revelation 2 we have the accusative use of the word *criteo.* One is holding us entirely, completely in His hand. I have a nickel in my hand. I'm holding it in the accusative sense of the Greek word. It is entirely, completely, totally in my hand. In the genitive use, it's just partially.

In John 10:27-29 Jesus said:

"My sheep hear my voice, and I know them, and they follow me: And I give unto them eternal life; and they shall never perish, neither shall any man pluck them out of my

hand. My Father, which gave them me, is greater than all; and no man is able to pluck them out of my Father's hand.''

I like the way the old black preacher gave the illustration. Because we are sealed by the Holy Spirit and in the hand of Christ and in the hand of God, he said, "If the Devil ever gets to our soul, he will have to come and break the seal of the Holy Spirit, pry open the hands of Christ, then pry open the hand of God; and I just don't believe he can do it!" There we are in the accusative use of the word *criteo*. We are held in the hand of Christ, and we shall never perish.

We Are Sealed by the Spirit

The believer can never be lost because he is sealed with the Holy Spirit. Let me read for you Ephesians 1:12-14:

"That we should be to the praise of his glory, who first trusted in Christ. In whom ye also trusted, after that ye heard the word of truth, the gospel of your salvation: in whom also after that ye believed, ye were sealed with that holy Spirit of promise, Which is the earnest of our inheritance until the redemption of the purchased possession, unto the praise of his glory.''

Every believer is sealed by the Holy Spirit. The moment one accepts Christ, that sealing takes place. The purpose of a seal is twofold: first, to indicate ownership; second, to guarantee safety.

When the United States government seal appears on something, you had better not tamper with it. It belongs to Uncle Sam. When the seal of the United States government appears, not only does that mean Uncle Sam owns it, but that he will do everything in his power to protect it. If it takes calling out the whole army, the navy, the air force, the marines, Uncle Sam will protect that which bears his seal.

That word *earnest* that we read means "to pledge." It is a down payment that guarantees the seller that the papers are all drawn up and cleared and the balance will be paid.

The Holy Spirit in your life and mine, sealing us, is God's down payment, God's earnest, God's pledge, God's token that He is going to finish that which He began when He redeemed the purchased possession—our bodies. Our souls are already saved, already redeemed. Then one day our bodies will be redeemed.

We can never be lost because we are sealed by the Holy Spirit.

Salvation Based on Blood Atonement

The believer can never be lost because his salvation is based on blood atonement. In Hebrews 9:11-14 we read:

"But Christ being come an high priest of good things to come, by a greater and more perfect tabernacle, not made with hands, that is to say, not of this building; Neither by the blood of goats and calves, but by his own blood he entered in once into the holy place, having obtained eternal redemption for us. For if the blood of bulls and of goats, and the ashes of an heifer sprinkling the unclean, sanctifieth to the purifying of the flesh: How much more shall the blood of Christ, who through the eternal Spirit offered himself without spot to God, purge your conscience from dead works to serve the living God?"

Two words I would have you note out of those verses: the first, *obtain*—"having obtained eternal redemption," perfect tense. He has obtained once for all our redemption. The word *purge* is in the present tense. It speaks of a continuous action. He continues yesterday, today, tomorrow and forever to purge us from our sins. *Having obtained*—perfect tense— "eternal redemption . . . ." He continues to purge us day by day from our sins.

Honesty of God

The believer can never be lost because his security is based on the honesty of God. Salvation is a gift. Romans 6:23 tells us the gift of God is salvation through Jesus Christ. We saw in Ephesians 2:8,9 that "it is the gift of God: Not of works, lest any man should boast." A gift is not earned. If I say to you, "I have a ten-dollar bill that I am going to give you. All you have to do is come and receive it," you would not be earning that ten-dollar bill. But if I say to you, "I have some work I would like for you to do, and if you'll do it at the time and place and in the right way, I'll give you ten dollars," then if you do it, you have earned the ten dollars.

Salvation is a gift. You and I cannot work for it. We cannot earn it. There is nothing we can do to merit or earn God's salvation. He gives it to us. "For God so loved the world that he gave his only begotten Son." "Thanks be unto God for his unspeakable gift." Now the honesty of God says to us, "You can never be lost." God will not take back that which He has given us. A wage can be forfeited. A gift is unconditional.

Conclusion

The believer can never be lost because Jesus prayed for our security, and His prayers are always answered. In John's Gospel, chapter 17, in His high priestly, intercessory, mediatorial prayer, Jesus asked for the believers two things: that they be kept from evil and that they be with Him in Heaven. In the final analysis, our security depends upon God answering the prayer of Jesus Christ. I believe that God answers His Son's prayer. Therefore, I conclude, a believer can never, never, never, never, never be lost because our security is in answer to Jesus' prayer.

12

THE BIBLE

and the Church

"Take heed therefore unto yourselves, and to all the flock, over the which the Holy Ghost hath made you overseers, to feed the church of God, which he hath purchased with his own blood."—Acts 20:28.

"Wives, submit yourselves unto your own husbands, as unto the Lord. For the husband is the head of the wife, even as Christ is the head of the church: and he is the saviour of the body. Therefore as the church is subject unto Christ, so let the wives be to their own husbands in every thing. Husbands, love your wives, even as Christ also loved the church, and gave himself for it; That he might sanctify and cleanse it with the washing of water by the word, That he might present it to himself a glorious church, not having spot, or wrinkle, or any such thing; but that it should be holy and without blemish. So ought men to love their wives

as their own bodies. He that loveth his wife loveth himself.
For no man ever yet hated his own flesh; but nourisheth
and cherisheth it, even as the Lord the church: For we are
members of his body, of his flesh, and of his bones. For this
cause shall a man leave his father and mother, and shall
be joined unto his wife, and they two shall be one flesh.
This is a great mystery: but I speak concerning Christ and
the church."—Eph. 5:22-32.

When we speak of the church, we speak of that which is
dearest to the heart of God. The church has a place in the
economy of God that no other organism or organization has.
The word for *church* in the Greek is *ekklesia,* meaning "a
called-out assembly." The late and imminent theologian, Dr.
B. H. Carroll, says that the word *ekklesia* appears no less
than 117 times in the New Testament. He goes on to say that,
with two or three exceptions, the word *ekklesia,* as it appears
in the New Testament, refers to a local, visible body of believers. So the church is a called-out assembly, local and visible, of baptized believers in the Lord Jesus Christ.

Appraisal of the Church

The only organism on earth that is empowered by a
heavenly power is the church. The only institution on earth
that is entrusted with the gospel message is the church. The
only body on earth that is engaged in a divine business is
the church.

The church reflects the heart of God, the hand of God, the
power of God, the love of God, the Spirit of God, the glory
of God, the Word of God, the work of God, the wisdom of God,
the might of God, the knowledge of God and the Son of God.

The church is a reservoir of truth. It is a repository of
wisdom. It is a refuge of safety.

The church can never be separated from Christ. The
church was created by His breath. The church is redeemed
by His blood. And the church is energized by His Spirit.

His mind is the church's thought. His heart is the church's love. His Spirit is the church's life.

The church is constituted by Christ, committed to Christ, empowered through Christ, and united in Christ.

We are body of His body, bone of His bone, flesh of His flesh.

If there were no church, there would be no New Testament, for the New Testament is a product of the church.

If there were no church, there would be no missions, for the worldwide missionary endeavor is a thrust and an outreach of the church.

If there were no church, there would be no baptism, for baptism is the doorway into the local assembly.

If there were no church, there would be no discipline of the believer, for it is the responsibility and the duty of the church to discipline the believer.

If there were no church, there would be no body of Christ, for the church is the body of Christ.

If there were no church, there would be no commission to evangelize, for it is the business of the church to evangelize.

If there were no church, there would be no pastor and no deacons, for the only institution in the world that has those two offices, pastor and deacon, is the church.

If you did away with the church, you would have to destroy the body of Christ, make void the promise of Christ and render powerless the blood of Christ. I read to you in my text, that He purchased the church with His own blood. I read to you that we are His body. I read to you that the church is subject to Christ, who is its glorified and exalted Head in Heaven.

I am of this persuasion: A man cannot love Christ without loving the church. How can a man love the Head when he doesn't love the body? A man cannot honor Christ without honoring the church. How can a man honor the Head, when he doesn't honor the body? A man cannot obey Christ when he does not abide by the teachings and doctrines and the precepts of the church. How can a man obey the Head when he disregards the rules and regulations of the body? I have met people, and so have you, who claim that they love Christ, but have no stock in and no part with the church. That is hard for me to reconcile.

I believe in the church. If you close the church, you will have to recall all the missionaries, silence all the preachers and cancel all public worship. If the church is wrong, the Bible is wrong. If the church is wrong, the Gospel is wrong. If the church is wrong, baptism is wrong. If the church is wrong, the Lord's supper is wrong. If the church is wrong, preaching is wrong. If the church is wrong, God is wrong. If the church is wrong, Christ is wrong. If the church is wrong, the Holy Spirit is wrong. If the church is wrong, the apostles were wrong. If the church is wrong, the early church fathers who gave their lives, burned at the stake, thrown to the wild animals, crucified upside down, are all wrong.

If the church is wrong, our fathers and our mothers were wrong. If the church is wrong, we are wrong. If the church is wrong, every principle the church endorses is wrong. If the church is wrong, every doctrine the church teaches is wrong. If the church is wrong, every truth the church espouses is wrong.

Someone might ask, "But why be so zealous about the church?" Here's why. If the church suffers, Christ suffers. If the church falters, Christ falters. If the church wavers, Christ wavers. If the church weakens, Christ weakens. If the church fails, Christ fails.

If anyone confronts you with the question: "What is right about the church?" tell him its *foundation* is right because it is built upon Christ. Tell him its *inflammation* is right because it is inflamed by the Holy Spirit. Tell him its *inspiration* is right because it is inspired by the Word of God. Tell him that its *declaration* is right because it declares the whole counsel of God. Tell him its *destination* is right because it is bound for the glory world. The church is right!

I am willing to stake all that I have and all that I ever might be for the church of God. This is our opportunity, our privilege, our testimony. This is our life, our heart, our soul. This is our dedication. The church of Jesus Christ is right. The church is such a marvelous thing. Its methods are *unimpeachable*. Its message is *unchangeable*. Its Master is *unconquerable*. Its multitudes are *uncountable*. Its majesty is *unparalleled*. Its might is *unequalled*. And its mission is *unmatched* in the world. This is the church, and it is a many-splendored thing.

The church depends more on prayer than it does on programs, promotions and projects.

Ladies and gentlemen, the church will never get on its feet until it first gets on its knees. Someone has said, "Satan trembles when he sees the weakest saint upon his knees." When it's the hardest to pray, we ought to pray the hardest. We can no more live without prayer than we can live without air because prayer is our source of power or channel of power from the Holy Spirit. When the church prays, it becomes *powerful*. And when it becomes powerful, it becomes *productive*. And when it becomes productive, it becomes *prosperous*. And when it becomes prosperous, it becomes *prominent*. And when the church becomes prominent, God is *glorified*, Christ is *magnified*, and the Gospel is *amplified*.

What is the greatest thing about the church? The greatest power of the church is the Holy Spirit. The greatest need of the church is dedicated members. The greatest burden of the church is soul winning. And the greatest privilege of the church is sharing Christ.

If your Christ is not worth sharing, He's not worth having. If your faith is not worth sharing, it's not worth having. If your church is not worth sharing, it's not worth your being a part of. This is the privilege of the church. The church is in a category all by itself. And the church must never be classified with any other organization on earth.

The church is the agent through which Christ carries on what He began while He was on earth in the days of His flesh. The church is the instrument through which Christ reaches out to the lost. The church is the salt through which Christ preserves the truth. The church is the light through which Christ lightens the darkened world. The church is the tool through which Christ makes bad men good and good men bad. This is the church.

Beyond a shadow of a doubt, the church is supreme. The church deserves first place in your life and mine. I would to God that we would give ourselves totally, unreservedly, unhesitatingly, to the ministry of the church.

When Christ was crucified, He was crucified for the church. When Christ commissioned, He commissioned the church. When Christ communicated, He communicated with the church. When Christ sent the Comforter, He sent the Comforter to the church. And beloved, when Christ comes again, He's coming for the church. This is the church of the living God.

Attitude Toward the Church

What should our attitude be toward the church? Because of its holiness, we should regard it with reverence. Because of its blessings, we should regard it with gratitude. Because of its sanctity, we should regard it with respect.

When I come on these church grounds, I feel much like Moses must have felt on yonder back side of the desert when he stood before the burning bush and when God said to him, "Moses, take off thy shoes from off thy feet, for the ground upon which thou standest is holy ground." This is holy ground, sanctified ground, God-bought ground, God-blessed ground, holy ground.

There was one church that Jesus bragged on. Which one? The church of Philadelphia, listed in the book of the Revelation. When Jesus instructed John to write to the churches, one was the church at Philadelphia, the church of brotherly love. Why did Jesus brag on this church? Because it was characterized by Christian love. It had a consecrated membership. It enjoyed a fervent prayer life. It was maintaining a worldwide missionary endeavor. It was operated by the principles of the blessed Book. And it waited patiently for the coming of the Lord Jesus Christ.

An Unusual Church

If someone were to ask you, "What is the most unusual church in history?" your answer would have to be, the church at Jerusalem. The church began as only a handful. In the upper room on the day of Pentecost, when the Holy Spirit came, there were only 120 members. Historians tell us that, during the days of the first century, the Jerusalem church grew from 50 to a membership of 75,000 people.

Talk about a super church! That was a super church. They had no cathedrals to house them, no capital to operate on; but they had the power of the Holy Spirit. They did not have television, but they had a clear channel to Heaven. They had no radio, yet they were tuned to the divine frequency. They had no telephone, yet they kept an open line of communication to the throne. They had no automobiles, yet they moved faster on their knees. They had no airplanes, yet they flew all over the world on wings of prayer. The most unusual church in history was empowered with and energized by the Holy Spirit.

What About Today?

Can we have such a church now? I believe we can, when we have the same fervor, the same dedication, the same compassion, the same love, the same energy and the same power. We have far greater advantages in our city than they had in Jerusalem. How many of you have ever been arrested on your way to church? How many of you have ever been taken out to a jail and put in a dungeon because you were a church member? You know what happened in the church at Jerusalem. They were so on fire for God, so sold out to Christ, so dedicated to evangelizing the city, that they cared not what others thought. It was an honor to be a Christian. It was an honor to be a member of the persecuted church.

What would bring revival to this church and churches like it all over our city, all over our nation and all over the world? It would not be great pulpiteers. It would not be worldwide coverage on television. It would not be a bank account that we could write out checks and buy buses and houses and buildings and land. The thing that will bring revival to our church is, if the Devil would so persecute us that some of us would have to seal our testimony in our own blood. This would bring growth, production and evangelism. This would bring a super church in Fort Worth. It might not be the biggest, but it would be the best. We need to follow the pattern of the New Testament in the book of Acts. The more they were persecuted, the more they grew. Growth always follows persecution.

I repeat: The church in Jerusalem was the most unusual church, yet they had not all these modern conveniences and communications that we have. But they did have the power of the Holy Spirit.

When we at this church come to the place where we love Christ more than we love comfort, where we love God more than we love gold, where we love souls more than we love silver, where we love Christ more than we love life, we will have a revival. We will have a revival when we get our hearts right with God. When we get right and go out into this community as flaming evangels, somebody is going to start criticizing and start persecuting, and we will grow all the more.

God, give us that kind of church! If it takes depression, God, send depression. Oh, I know some of you say, "Well, you didn't live in the days of the Depression." I was born in it. I surely did live in it. But I know this: When people stood in bread lines, they also stood in prayer lines and in church lines. If it takes that, God, give us a depression and a church that suffers for Christ. Let's get serious for Christ.

Let us observe three things now about the church: first,

The Foundation of the Church

The church had its origin in Christ. There was no church in the Old Testament. There was no church in the wilderness. The church was a mystery until the day of Christ. Any church before Christ was too early. And any church after Christ is too late. Listen to the testimony of Jesus Himself in Matthew 16:18: "Thou art Peter [*Petros*, the small stone], and upon this rock [*Petra*, the large stone] I will build my church; and the gates of hell shall not prevail against it." It is His church. It is His body. It is His blood. It is His breath. It is His business. Jesus Christ is Founder and foundation of the church.

If the church was founded by Christ in the days of His flesh, as we believe it was, what, then, happened on the day of Pentecost? First, the church was empowered by the Holy Spirit, in keeping with the promise of Christ, "I will not leave you comfortless, but I will send you another comforter." The church, second, was strengthened by the addition of three thousand members. Why, that's more than most churches have in a lifetime. They had that many in one day because the Holy Spirit empowered them and empowered their preacher. Do you know what I think the secret of that was? The upper room. They prayed, they tarried, they waited for ten long days. We won't have revival until we learn to pray.

When Peter got up to preach on the day of Pentecost, the power of God came down. The prayers of the saints had gone up, so the power of God came down, and they had a mighty revival, and three thousand souls were added in one day.

Since the day of its beginning with Christ upon the earth, nothing has been added. The church has always had two ordinances: baptism and the Lord's supper. The church as always had two offices: pastor and deacon. The church has always had one message: salvation by grace plus nothing and minus nothing. The church has always had one mission: winning the lost. The church has always had one creed: Christ. The church has always had one law: love. The church has always had one administrator: the Holy Spirit. The church has always had one book: the Bible. The church has always had one head: Christ. The church has always had one hope: the second coming of Jesus.

Let us observe, second,

The Function of the Church

The church has the most important and most unique function in all the world. It is entrusted with a priceless treasure—the Gospel of redeeming grace. It is involved in a universal business—evangelizing the world. It is empowered by a divine Person—the Holy Spirit.

The church's function obligates the church to the world. The church's function is not to socialize or organize or harmonize, but to agonize, evangelize and baptize. And beloved, the church has but two choices: evangelize or fossilize. The church can meet its obligation to the world only as we meet our obligation to the church.

Perhaps we ought to take inventory. If everybody had given the same amount to the church this year that you gave, how could we have operated? How could the church have turned its lights on and opened its doors? How could the church have operated if everybody had attended to the same degree of regularity that you have attended? How could the church have had power this year if everybody had prayed no more than you have prayed? How could the church have won any souls if every member had won the same number that you have won? I repeat: The church cannot meet its obligation to the world until we meet our obligation to the church.

You and I can meet our obligation to the church as we exalt its Head, extend its boundary, enhance its beauty, enlarge its facilities and ennoble its status. These things can be done as you first strengthen the church with your prayers, support the church with your purse and sanction the church with your presence. Think it over.

Most churches and most members boast of being fundamentally sound. About the only thing sound about some church members is their sleep. The church is filled with willing people—the majority are willing to sit back and let the minority do all the giving, going, praying, visiting and working. And when things aren't going too well, they blame it on others. And when the church is moving forward, they take the credit.

That reminds me of the story of the elephant and the flea. When they walked across the bridge together, the bridge shook. When they got on the other side, the little flea looked up at the elephant and said, "Boy, *we* sure did shake that bridge!" Which are you, an elephant or a flea, when it comes to the work of Christ?

We operate our homes, our businesses, our pleasures, our entertainments and have everything we want; then if there's anything left over, we might invest it in the church. That's wrong! And you know, just coming to church doesn't mean that you're altogether right with God and that you're altogether involved in the church's ministry. Some people, who sit on these pews every week, couldn't care less about a soul in Africa or China or Mexico or even next door. The time has come when we must mean business with God.

A good motto for the church would be: Let's wake up, sing up, pray up, pay up, stay up and never give up, let up or shut up until the cause of Christ is built up.

Perhaps we do well to ask ourselves a question: If every member of my church were just like me, what kind of church would my church be?

Finally, we observe

The Future of the Church

The outlook for this whole world is dark, dismal, discouraging. We must not look around us, or we'll be discouraged.

We must not look within us, or we will despair. We must look above us; then we'll be encouraged when we think of our future.

Civil strife at home, economic crises abroad. Our land, our economy are in trouble. Our educational system, our judicial system are in trouble. Our governmental system is in trouble. Our city is in trouble. Our homes are in trouble. There is trouble on every hand. The Bible says that in the end time there shall come wars and rumors of wars. The Bible says that in the end time there shall come a terrible period called the Period of Tribulation. The Bible says that in the end time the Antichrist shall take over and rule the world.

But, thank God, we're not looking for war; we're looking for the Prince of Peace. Thank God, we're not looking for the Tribulation; we're looking for Glory. We're not looking for Antichrist; we're looking for Jesus. We're not looking for death; we're looking for life. We're not looking for the undertaker; we're looking for the "Up-taker." Oh, what a future is ours! I do not believe the church will suffer the pangs and horrors of the Tribulation Period because in chapter 4 of the Revelation it is taken up; then it doesn't appear until chapter 19, when it comes back with Jesus.

What a fabulous time!

"Let not your heart be troubled: ye believe in God, believe also in me. In my Father's house are many mansions: if it were not so, I would have told you. I go to prepare a place for you. And if I go and prepare a place for you, I will come again, and receive you unto myself; that where I am, there ye may be also."— John 14:1-3.

I think that I shall never see a church that's all it ought to be,
A church whose members never stray beyond the straight and narrow way;
A church that has no empty pews, whose pastor never has the blues;
A church whose deacons always "deac," and none is proud, and all are meek;

**Where gossips never peddle lies and make complaints or
criticize;**
**Where all are sweet and kind and all to others' faults are
blind.**
**Such perfect churches there may be, but none of them are
known to me.**
**But still we'll work and pray and plan to make our church
the best we can.**

Conclusion

Everything I have, I owe to the church. I will be indebted
all the days of my life to the church. If there had never been
a church, humanly speaking, I would have never been saved.
If there had never been a church, I would have never been
baptized, because I was saved and baptized in the church.
If there had never been a church, I would have never been
educated, because I was educated by the church. If there had
never been a church, I would have never been ordained, because I was ordained by the church. If there had never been
a church, I would not have a wife, because I was married in
the church. If there had never been a church, I would have
no ministry, because my ministry is the ministry of the
church. If there had never been a church, I would have no
anchor for my life and soul. My past, my present and my
future are anchored in the church.

It's in the Book—the Bible and the church!

13

THE BIBLE

and You

"When I consider thy heavens, the work of thy fingers, the moon and the stars, which thou hast ordained; What is man, that thou art mindful of him? and the son of man, that thou visitest him?"—Ps. 8:3,4.*

I'm happy to report that, if you were the only person on this earth, God would have a plan, a program, a blueprint for your life. You are in the mind of God at all times.

In Psalm 121 the psalmist says:

"I will lift up mine eyes unto the hills, from whence cometh my help. My help cometh from the Lord, which made heaven and earth. He will not suffer thy foot to be moved: he that keepeth thee will not slumber. Behold, he that keepeth Israel shall neither slumber nor sleep. The Lord is thy keeper: the Lord is thy shade upon thy right hand.

The sun shall not smite thee by day, nor the moon by night.
The Lord shall preserve thee from all evil: he shall preserve
thy soul. The Lord shall preserve thy going out and thy
coming in from this time forth, and even for evermore."

Your Place in the Bible

The same God who presides over the destinies of nations, cares for you. God is just as concerned about the conflict in your life as He is about the conflict in the Middle East or Vietnam or Rhodesia or Northern Ireland or anywhere else where there are conflicts. Did you know you are written up in the Bible? The Bible is written to you and about you. It records your past, your present and your future. It speaks of your birth, your life, your death. When the Bible speaks of creation, it speaks of your creation. When the Bible speaks of life, it speaks of your life. When the Bible speaks of death, it speaks of your death. The Bible is God's Word to God's people in every age.

There are those in the school of higher criticism who would have us believe the Bible is for yesteryear, another epic, another era, another age, another time, another people. But God's Word is as old as time and as new as tomorrow. The Word of God is just as fresh as the dewdrops of the morning. No wonder the psalmist said, "Thy word have I hid in mine heart, that I might not sin against thee." No wonder Paul said, "For the word of God is quick, and powerful, and sharper than any twoedged sword." No wonder the psalmist said the Word is "sweeter than honey and the honeycomb."

The Bible is speaking *to* you and *about* you. Your picture, your portrait, your life, your time upon the earth are recorded in this Book.

The Bible is such a remarkable Book. While you are reading it, it is reading you. While you are examining it, it is examining you. The Bible knows your thoughts, your motives, your desires, your intents, your plans and your program for your life. The Bible knows who you are and from where you came. The Bible knows why you are here and where you are at this moment. The Bible knows where you're going and how you're going to get there.

How Much Are You Worth?

The Word of God depicts your life, describes your heart. Jeremiah said, "The heart is deceitful above all things, and desperately wicked: who can know it?" The Bible divulges your motives, discerns your thoughts, defines your mission in life. The Bible dissolves your doubts, destroys your fears, declares your worth and designates your destiny. All men are headed either to Heaven with Christ or to an eternal Hell without Christ. The Bible makes it clear that all men of Adam's race are traveling one of these two roads.

By the way, who said you were worth only 98 cents in chemical compound? The Bible speaks more of you than that; besides, in your actual worth, I understand that every pound of your body has an energy potential of 11,400,000 kilowatts of atomic energy. And atomic energy does not come cheaply. Atomic energy is worth 570 million dollars a pound. If you weigh in at 150 pounds, you are worth 85 billion dollars, and some of you—well, you're worth a bit more!

The Bible tells me that one day we who are born again will rule and reign with Christ upon the earth for a thousand years. We're somebody in God's estimate.

God loved you enough to send His Son to die on the cross for your sins. God loves you enough to give you a Book. God loves you enough to send His Spirit to be your Comforter, your Guide, your constant Companion. God loves you enough to build in Heaven a wonderful place for you, where you will spend eternity.

Your life basically is in two segments: today and eternity. Where you spend eternity will depend on how you prepare today. The Gospel of Jesus Christ is written in the Bible, but you and I are writing a gospel every day.

The gospel according to you is read both far and wide.
There are some things in life that you simply cannot hide.
The gospel according to you has words and deeds galore;
And, like the rubbish of the ocean, they wash upon the shore.
The gospel according to you must never, never be a lie,
For the truth will be revealed before you come down to die.

Now what is the gospel according to you? What do men see when they look at your life, your character, your conduct and when they listen to your conversation? Jesus said, "Let your light so shine before men, that they may see your good works, and glorify your Father which is in heaven." Every time an unsaved man looks at your life and mine, he gets some sort of impression of Christ, some kind of impression of the church and Christianity. There are some things in life we just cannot hide. We're writing a gospel every day that we live.

Basic Relationships

In your life and experiences, there are several basic relationships. You have a relationship with yourself, and that relationship is very vital. You have a relationship with your family, your friends, your enemies, your critics and with your God.

The proper relationship with yourself depends basically on quieting your internal conflicts. There are some basic difficulties, problems and inner conflicts that you and God alone can handle. So to have the right relationship with yourself, you must learn to quiet your inner conflicts.

The proper relationship with your family depends upon controlling your external conflicts. Our homes ought not be armed camps nor battlefronts. They ought to be places of love, understanding, compassion, kindness, patience and forbearance one to another.

The proper relationship with your friends depends on your adjusting your social behavior. There are some ways you can behave when you are by yourself, but you can't behave that way out in the circle of life. Some things you must curtail, drop from your life, in order to have the proper relationship with your friends.

If you're to have the proper relationship with your critics, you must first learn to analyze your own self. At times we wonder why people talk about us, criticize us; but if we would take a long look in the looking glass of God's Word, we might know why.

The proper relationship with your enemies depends upon incorporating Christian principles. The flesh says, "Get even." The flesh says, "Knock him down again." The flesh says, "Lord, pour out a hailstorm upon his crop." The flesh says, "Lord, let him have four flat tires this week." The flesh says, "Lord, let him have trouble in his home next week. Let him have trouble on the job next week." That's not the Christian spirit! Jesus commands, "Love your enemies." When we do, we'll have the right relationship with our enemies.

Your proper relationship with God depends upon your acceptance of His Son as your personal Saviour. No way can you appease God except by trusting His Son Jesus Christ. Nothing you can do with your hands, with your feet, with your body or with your life will bring you into the proper relationship with God. You must have Christ in your heart and life.

Let me underscore your relationship to God. Your relationship to God depends not upon your thinking nor upon your feeling but upon your believing. The Bible says, "He that believeth . . . ." Someone comes back with, "But, pastor, I don't understand it." That's the marvel of grace. God doesn't require you to understand it. He simply demands you to believe it. That is the right relationship to God.

Portraits of Life

You have several portraits of your life.

There is, first, a self portrait. This is a portrait of how you see yourself. Nobody else sees you like you see yourself.

Then there is the portrait of your friends. In this portrait your friends are looking at you. You see yourself the way your friends see you.

Then the third portrait is God's portrait. How does God see you? You see yourself basically on the inside. Your friends see you basically on the outside. But God sees both sides— inside and outside. There are some things we can cover up from our families. There are some things we can strike out of the portrait from our friends. If we try hard enough, we can almost fool ourselves once in awhile. But we're not fooling God. God sees not as man sees, because man looks on the outward appearance, but God looks on the heart.

Look at the portrait that you have of yourself. Are you satisfied with it? Look at the portrait that your friends have of you. Are you acceptable to them? Look at the portrait that God has of you—and this is the most important. Is God satisfied with the portrait He sees of your life?

Somebody says, "I don't seem to get much out of life anymore." You will never get any more out of life than you put into life. The dividends that your life pays will depend upon the initial investment that you make. The poet put it this way:

> **I bargained with life for a penny,**
> **And life would pay no more,**
> **However I begged that evening**
> **When I counted my scanty store;**
> **For life is a just employer:**
> **He gives you what you ask;**
> **But once you've set the wage,**
> **You must bear the task.**

Don't expect any more out of life than you're willing to put into it. Do you want to know how you can solve life's riddles? Apply God's wisdom. Do you want to know how you can overcome the world? Believe God's Word. Do you want to know how you can become prosperous? Seek first the kingdom of God and His righteousness. Do you want to know how you can conquer your fears? Embrace God's love. The Bible says, "Perfect love casteth out fear." Do you want to know how you can endure life's hardships? Receive God's grace. Do you want to know how you can accomplish life's mission? Utilize God's strength, and say with Paul, when facing that task tomorrow, "I can do all things through Christ which strengtheneth me." Do you want to know how you can abide forever? Do God's will. Do you want to know how you can be saved from sin? Accept God's Son.

What Is Our Life?

What is your life? Your life is a race. Run it well.

Your life is a journey. Travel with care.

Your life is a book. Write every chapter as though it might be the last one. You may have already eaten your last breakfast. You may have already heard your last Sunday school lesson. You may have already heard the last song your ears will ever hear. You may have already punched the clock for the last time. I repeat: your life is a book. Write every chapter as though it might be the last chapter.

Your life is a poem. Make every stanza rhyme.

Your life is a story. Tell it like it is.

Your life is a battle. Put on the whole armor of God that you may be able to stand against the wiles of the Devil.

Your life is a grindstone. Whether your life grinds you down or polishes you up will depend upon the stuff you're made of.

What is your life? The purpose of your life must be based on God's will. The philosophy of your life must be found in God's Word. The power of your life must be furnished by God's Spirit. If you are a Christian, your life belongs to God. A Christian is alive to a new way of life. If you are a Christian, live like it, look like it, speak like it, walk like it, think like it and act like it. A Christian is a Christian is a Christian—not on Sunday only. Monday morning religion is good, too.

When you get out there on the job and things seem to be

piling up on you and your wires get a little bit crossed up because everything went wrong at breakfast and everything went wrong on the way to work and everything seems to be going wrong at work, don't forget that the same Christ who lives on Sunday lives on Monday, and the same infused life of Christ is in you on Monday as was in you on Sunday.

Your life is a life that Christ is living through. This does not mean you are perfect. I've met a few in life who said, "Well, since I've been saved, I've never sinned." I just mark it down right there: *sin number one,* because lying is a sin. Some of us might look like angels, but not many of us act like angels. Do you see any wings sprouting out anywhere? There is no such thing as perfection for mortals. But, beloved, you can be on the road to perfection.

A man's journey to perfection may be compared to a man going from Dallas to Miami. He gets in the car and out on the highway. He is not in Miami, but he is on the road to Miami. When a man gets saved, he gets on board the old gospel train and starts the Glory run. He is not in Heaven, but he is on the way to Heaven. We're not perfect, but we're on the road to perfection.

The moment you were saved, you stepped into a new world. "If any man be in Christ, he is a new creature." You have a home in Heaven. Because you are a Christian, you have been delivered from eternal death, from eternal separation, from eternal judgment, from eternal perdition. A Christian is free—free from the law of sin and death, free from the power of sin, free from the penalty of sin, and one day we will be free from the presence of sin.

Two Kinds of People

There are two kinds of people, the saved and the unsaved. If you are unsaved, you are blind, undone, hopeless, helpless, apart from God and Christ, dead in trespasses and sin. If you are unsaved, you are destined to spend eternity without Christ. You are bound for the regions of the damned in the lake of fire that burns forever. If you are unsaved, you are condemned to judgment and consigned to eternal death. The Bible declares, "The wages of sin is death, but the gift of God is eternal life." The Bible declares, "The soul that sinneth, it shall die." The Bible declares, "When lust hath conceived, it bringeth forth sin: and sin, when it is finished, bringeth forth death."

But wait! You don't have to go on unsaved. God loves you. Jesus Christ died for you. You don't have to be lost. You don't have to die in your sins. You don't have to face God at the judgment bar. You can change all that right now by trusting Christ in your heart. You can be saved by simply receiving Him into your life.

There are two people who know what your life is like, you and God. To everybody else your life may seem a hidden mystery, but God knows and you know. If you and God are both satisfied with your life as it is, nothing can be done for you. There is nothing I can offer you and nothing God can do for you. But if you're not satisfied and God is not satisfied, there's hope for you. You can do something about it. But whatever you plan to do about your life, you'd best do now; for the Bible warns, "Boast not thyself of to morrow." God warns, "My spirit will not always strive with man." Today is your day of salvation.

If you believe God is dissatisfied with your life, then I invite you to do something about it. Surely you're not satisfied. If you're outside the church and need a church home where you can worship and serve, surely you know you have a need and are not satisfied. If your life is not counting for Christ, not shining for the Lord day by day, on the job and off the job, Sunday and Monday, then surely you're not totally satisfied. Remember, you're writing a gospel every day.

The Bible and you. What about it? Are you satisfied? More importantly, is God satisfied?

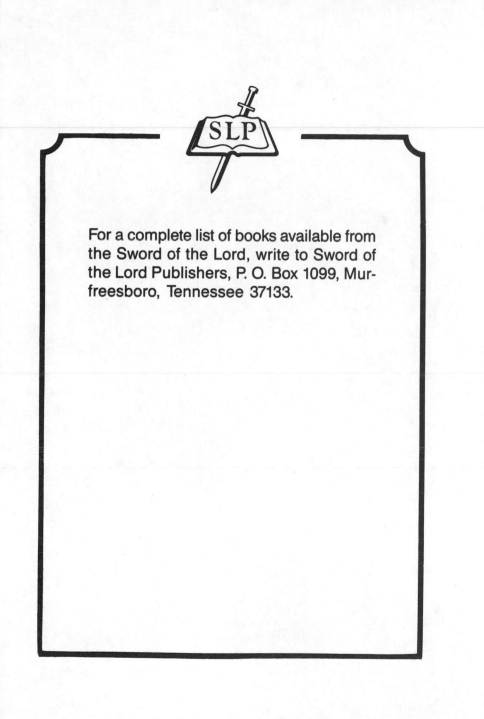

For a complete list of books available from the Sword of the Lord, write to Sword of the Lord Publishers, P. O. Box 1099, Murfreesboro, Tennessee 37133.